AN EVOLUTIONARY PSYCHOLOGY OF LEADER-FOLLOWER RELATIONS

AN EVOLUTIONARY PSYCHOLOGY OF LEADER-FOLLOWER RELATIONS

PATRICK MCNAMARA
AND
DAVID TRUMBULL

Nova Science Publishers, Inc.
New York

For permission to use material from this book please contact us:
Telephone 631-231-7269; Fax 631-231-8175
Web Site: http://www.novapublishers.com

NOTICE TO THE READER

The Publisher has taken reasonable care in the preparation of this book, but makes no expressed or implied warranty of any kind and assumes no responsibility for any errors or omissions. No liability is assumed for incidental or consequential damages in connection with or arising out of information contained in this book. The Publisher shall not be liable for any special, consequential, or exemplary damages resulting, in whole or in part, from the readers' use of, or reliance upon, this material.

Independent verification should be sought for any data, advice or recommendations contained in this book. In addition, no responsibility is assumed by the publisher for any injury and/or damage to persons or property arising from any methods, products, instructions, ideas or otherwise contained in this publication.

This publication is designed to provide accurate and authoritative information with regard to the subject matter covered herein. It is sold with the clear understanding that the Publisher is not engaged in rendering legal or any other professional services. If legal or any other expert assistance is required, the services of a competent person should be sought. FROM A DECLARATION OF PARTICIPANTS JOINTLY ADOPTED BY A COMMITTEE OF THE AMERICAN BAR ASSOCIATION AND A COMMITTEE OF PUBLISHERS.

LIBRARY OF CONGRESS CATALOGING-IN-PUBLICATION DATA
Available upon request

ISBN 978-1-60456-600-0

Published by Nova Science Publishers, Inc. ✦ New York

CONTENTS

Chapter 1

EVOLUTIONARY PSYCHOLOGY APPROACHES TO THE PHENOMENON OF THE LEADER

INTRODUCTION

Everyone knows that 'leaders' can bring great benefits and great harm to a people—indeed to the world. Yet very little solid scientific knowledge is available on these individuals. There are now collections of essays on the latest findings in the science of leadership but readers of these essays soon discover that the bulk of the findings in the field boil down to loose descriptive studies of people generally acknowledged as leaders of one kind or another. More ambitious studies attempt to model leadership via collection of huge amounts of descriptive measurements on individuals who score high on some putative leadership trait. But the strategy is fundamentally the same in both types of studies: First, you identify groups of individuals who most people agree are leaders and then you study them intensively in order to discover what makes them tick. There is of course nothing wrong with this sort of approach. It is data-driven and certainly necessary if any science of leadership is to emerge. But other forms of study are necessary as well. In particular, theory is necessary and may be helpful in generating new approaches to the study of leadership.

"Leadership studies" at present, however, are data rich and theory poor. It is our contention that the field of leadership studies would benefit from an infusion of theoretical appraisals from evolutionary psychology. Evolutionary psychology has both imported theoretical tools from organismal evolutionary biology and has itself devised some new theoretical tools that are especially suited for the study of leaders. The 'leader', we contend, has both shaped and been shaped by the forces of biologic and cultural evolution that have shaped human evolutionary history itself. The leader has put his stamp on human evolutionary processes and thereby shaped what it is to be human.

We hasten to add that we do not believe that there is a 'leader gene' or that people are born or biologically prepared to be gullible and passive 'followers' of 'strong leaders' who are somehow biologically or culturally superior to the followers and so forth. Instead, our research and theoretical stance suggests that every individual is born with the capacity to lead other individuals in enterprises of real consequence. Why some individuals realize that capacity and others do not is a theme we will address throughout this book. But the data do suggest that most people at some point in their lives can function as pretty effective leaders – at least in some local social context.

These sorts of local leadership roles carry real fitness consequences for both leaders and followers. All other things being equal, the better the leader the greater the success of the enterprise under consideration. When an enterprise is successful the kinds of benefits that accrue to both the leader and the groups include better access to greater resources, greater prestige, increased opportunities for future leadership positions in the local group and so forth.

When we move from the case of small group, local context leadership situations to more large scale leadership enterprises involving thousands and perhaps millions of people the dynamics of leadership, not surprisingly, change in important ways. Obviously the stakes are higher and the potential benefits correspondingly higher. No less obvious is the fact that the corresponding risks are higher as well. If you were born into the 20th century, then you do not need us to explain that there are risks associated with following 'strong leaders'. The twenty-first century, unfortunately, looks likes it will be no better in terms of production of lethal and bloodthirsty leaders. The risks of ignorance about who becomes leaders and why are tremendous, involving the possibility of prolonged and tremendous suffering for huge numbers of people and even perhaps the untimely death of millions of human beings in war or some other misguided political project. While it cannot be claimed that the leader alone is responsible for the lives of all of these millions of peoples, it can be argued that he more than any other single individual was/is in a position to tip the balance in favor of one option over another.

The study of the leader then should not be the preserve of just a single discipline (like history or political science). Instead, all of the human sciences should attempt to contribute to developing an understanding of the leader. Our effort in the present work is to help stimulate evolutionary psychology approaches to the study of the leader.

Our fundamental claim in the present monograph is that a *leader* or better, 'wise leadership' is central to the establishment of cooperation and order in any human group or society. Conversely a poor or unscrupulous leader is central to production of disorder in human societies. Two styles of leadership are identified: 1) a prestige oriented style where the leader attains his leadership position via a sterling reputation for high moral character, high intelligence and high accomplishment. 2) a dominance-oriented strategy where the leader attains his leadership position via an ability to politically manipulate and dominate his opponents and to use force when necessary to do so. Many individuals attempt to alternate between the two styles but this is a difficult balancing act to say the least. Both styles of leadership find their evolutionary roots in the need to develop cooperative enterprises by developing systems of trust between individuals with differing genetic interests as well as by punishing free-riders or individuals who seek to benefit from cooperative enterprises without contributing any of the work required to succeed in these cooperative enterprises.

In order to get a cooperative enterprise off the ground and depending on the size of a given social group one person (or one relatively small group of people) has to take responsibility for proposing goals (that enlists the support of the group), and of finding ways to reach those goals. The extent to which those goals are reached with minimal costs is the measure of success of the leader. The leader enriches the lives of the persons in the cooperative group and is then rewarded by members of that group and so his or her fitness is increased accordingly. Followers in these sort of small scale cooperative enterprises are 'followers' with respect to the aforementioned agreed upon goals. Once the goals are achieved the so-called followers may themselves become leaders with respect to a new or different set of goals. This ongoing and ever-changing set of leader-follower relationships, coalitions and cooperative enterprises creates the context for the establishment of order and cooperation in relatively small-scale human societies.

The history of humankind has shown that the process of leadership typically breaks down and all too often with serious or even catastrophic consequences. Hence there is a need to study the ways in which leadership works. What are its evolutionary roots? What is the nature of leadership? Are leaders made by circumstances or by biology or some interaction of the two? What about followers? Can every follower become a good leader given the right conditions? What forces promote wise leadership and what forces lead to breakdowns in leadership?

Factors such as leader intelligence, dominance, affiliation need, achievement orientation, personality traits, genetics, and every other conceivable variable have been tested as potential predictor variables in the leadership literature.

Although relationships between these predictor variables and various measures of leadership have often been reported, no evolutionary psychological theoretical models have yet been proposed to account for these relationships.

Like the ancient biographer Plutarch, the modern scholar James McGregor Burns (Burns, 1978) drew upon his studies of presidents and social movement leaders, to highlight two important dimensions of leadership – that leadership was relational and that the motivations of leaders and followers were keys to understanding leadership and change. Burns also insisted that great leadership had moral dimensions. He thus made a distinction between two different but compatible leadership behaviors -- transforming and transactional. He defined transactional leadership as the process whereby one person takes the initiative in making contact with others for the purpose of an exchange of valued things. Transformational leadership had a greater moral content in that it transformed followers into moral agents and leaders in their own right. We will show that some of the same lessons on leadership (indeed even greater lessons) can be found in the ancient Greek philosopher and biographer Plutarch.

Plutarch was a Greek living, teaching, and writing in the Roman Empire in the second century of our era. The aim of his successful school of rhetoric and philosophy was to turn juveniles into adults with the intellectual and moral strength to be leaders. His theory of the dynamics of leadership is worked out and illustrated in his series of biographies of dozens of leaders of the classical age. He argued that imitation or emulation of the moral and intellectual virtues of others could trigger leadership skills in anyone who had a little ambition. Our reading of Plutarch suggests that he developed a sophisticated analysis of the dynamics of social emulation in service to acquiring eminence and leadership skills. We therefore begin with an analysis of Plutarch's insights into emulation and leadership. We then summarize the scientific literature on emulation in so far as it relates to the potential role of emulation in leadership theory. We then conclude this chapter with recommendations on how to incorporate emulation as a focus into future leadership studies.

As is the case now, the classical world had its conventional formats for biographies. Plutarch, however, abandoned the conventional emphasis on the great battles and momentous turns of fate to focus, instead, on the moral character and leadership abilities of his subject. He tells us in beginning his Life of Alexander:

> "It must be borne in mind that my design is not to write histories, but lives. And the most glorious exploits do not always furnish us with the clearest discoveries of virtue or vice in men; sometimes a matter of less moment, an expression or a jest, informs us better of their characters and inclinations, than the most famous sieges, the greatest armaments, or the bloodiest battles whatsoever." --Life of Alexander, 1

Plutarch breaks new ground by using the actions and accomplishments not as the subject of his writings but as means of probing the character of his subject, the man or woman who rises to become a successful leader. In this manner, Plutarch lays out his analysis of leadership dynamics in his "Parallel Lives" (Plutarch, Clough, 2001).

For each of the great men of ancient Greece and Rome, Plutarch wrote a Life; 50 of them survive. Interestingly, in his lives of the great men of the classical age he also made a point of telling the stories of many of the great women of the age as well. Indeed, in nearly every one of the surviving Lives of the men, there is some major female figure such as Agiatis who gave herself as a hostage to the enemies of Sparta in order to save Sparta (Life of Cleomenes), Cornelia mother and teacher of the great reformers of the Roman republic, the Gracchi (Life of Caius Gracchus and Life of Tiberius Gracchus); Porcia who as wife of Brutus matched her husband in fierce opposition to tyranny and died at her own hand rather than live as the subject of a tyrant (Life of Marcus Brutus); Volumnia, mother of Coriolanus who saved the city of Rome from the armies commanded by her son (Life of Coriolanus); Cleopatra who conceived an empire centered on the eastern Mediterranean and Egypt (Life of Caesar) but failed when she allied herself with the tragically flawed Antony (Life of Marc Antony). Additionally, Plutarch produced a tract on the *Arete* (a Greek word variously translated as "virtue" "excellence" or "bravery") of Women in which he sets forth 28 specific historical instances of women founding cities, defeating enemies in battle, establishing justice and restoring domestic tranquility. Plutarch had carried on a long and satisfying intellectual exchange with his close friend and female academic colleague Clea. He addressed his *Virtues of Women* to her as an extended treatment of a philosophical position he had posited for her consideration, namely that man's virtues and women's virtues are one and the same. It was, at the time, a somewhat unorthodox position for a Greek philosopher to take. But Plutarch was once again breaking with classical tradition and anticipating modern thought which finds the inner workings of the psyche more revelatory of the man (or woman) than does the accidents of birth on which the ancients placed inordinate value.

In the Lives, Plutarch's basic method was to compare a Greek with a Roman. Thus, Solon, the Athenian lawgiver, is paired with Poplicola, author of the constitution of the Roman Republic. Each, the Grecian and the Roman, had much to commend him; each was also flawed as are all human beings. The contrast between the two leader's accomplishments and mistakes when facing roughly analogous personal, political or military challenges helped Plutarch to bring into sharp focus the utility and inner workings of leadership dynamics.

Plutarch wrote the Lives of the noble Greeks and Romans and his Virtues of Women to inspire others to emulate the lives of these leaders. Plutarch wanted to incite his readers (and himself) to greatness and nobility of character.

> "It was for the sake of others that I first commenced writing biographies; but I find myself proceeding and attaching myself to it for my own purposes; the virtues of these great

men serving me as a sort of looking-glass, in which I may see how to adjust and adorn my own life". --Life of Timoleon, prologue

Like many of his contemporaries Plutarch believed that the path to excellence in leadership lay in the *emulation of a worthy model.*

"It becomes a man's duty to pursue and make after the best and choicest of everything, that he may not only employ his contemplation, but may also be improved by it. For as that color is most suitable to the eye whose freshness and pleasantness stimulates and strengthens the sight, so a man ought to apply his intellectual perception to such objects as, with the sense of delight, are apt to call it forth, and allure it to its own proper good and advantage.

"Such objects we find in the acts of virtue, which also produce in the minds of mere readers about them, an emulation and eagerness that may lead them on to imitation. In other things there does not immediately follow upon the admiration and liking of the thing done, any strong desire of doing the like...

"But virtue, by the bare statement of its actions, can so affect men's minds as to create at once both admiration of the things done and desire to imitate the doers of them. The goods of fortune we would possess and would enjoy; those of virtue we long to practice and exercise; we are content to receive the former from others, the latter we wish others to experience from us. Moral good is a practical stimulus; it is no sooner seen, than it inspires an impulse to practice; and influences the mind and character not by a mere imitation which we look at, but, by the statement of the fact, creates a moral purpose which we form...And so we have thought fit to spend our time and pains in writing of the lives of famous persons..." --Life of Pericles, 1-2

In the Lives, Plutarch gives us many examples of men who became leaders themselves by emulating the leaders who went before them. So we see Julius Caesar emulating the life of Alexander the Great and the brilliant Roman general Marius framing his manner of life and command on that of Scipio Africanus Minor, the vanquisher of Rome's long-time enemy, Carthage.

In his 'Lives' and in the several volumes of collected essays and reflections called the 'Moralia', Plutarch wrote often on Greek paideia or education. The goal of education he argued was to attain to nobility of character. The way to achieve nobility of character was to find a worthy teacher and then to emulate the virtues of that teacher. Plutarch repeatedly emphasized the need to seek out worthy models, leaders of great moral character, in order to attain to honor, glory and leadership. He suggested that readers and seekers identify worthy models and then to approach them confidently and explicitly ask them to become their students. This method of finding a worthy teacher/mentor and then becoming that teacher's disciple was standard among individuals in the ancient world seeking to learn philosophy and rhetoric in order to become leaders. Plutarch recommended extensions of the method to the political realm in order to raise up worthy political leaders.

Plutarch in writing his Lives seems to employ a set of principles concerning the making of virtuous leaders and he uses the lives to illustrate these universal principles. He has a theory of leadership which is then applied to the Lives he studies and summarizes. Here are the major principles he uses:

1. (Effects of father presence/absence) If the leader is born into an illustrious family he seeks always to live up to the good repute of his ancestors; if of humble origins he considers it his duty to leave his family name as illustrious on his death as that of any family in his commonwealth. In either event, he will advance on his own talent and initiative for it is often the case that the leader has lost his father while yet a youth. Death of a father can trigger extraordinary ability in a youth if that youth has some acquired or innate virtue to build upon…otherwise father absence is detrimental to later achievement.

2. (Effects of ambition) A leader displays, from earliest youth, a passion for distinction and a genius for greatness.

3. (Effects of a liberal education) A leader benefits from the broadening effects of a liberal education, in particular becoming a master of persuasive speaking or rhetoric which he uses to organize and inspire his followers.

4. (Effects of local models) A leader finds worthy models to emulate, so that if he has seen further it is "by standing on the shoulders of Giants." And he does this without descending into destructive envy, seeing in the excellence of others, a model to strive toward, rather than a rival and threat. He, moreover, deflects the envy of others who, seeing his rise as leader, might be tempted to topple him.

5. (Effects of planning and vision) A leader develops plans for the world he wants to build. They are big, bold, and ambitious. They may extend beyond his own life on earth. The leader effectively infuses others with the desire to be part of that plan, and he anticipates his opponent's responses.

6. (Effects of character strengths) The leader, in his relation to others consistently practices the cardinal virtues of justice, prudence, temperance, and fortitude.

7. (Effects of a philosophy of Life and Death) The leader, when his time comes, dies nobly, leaving a world that has been changed for the better by his actions.

In this book we will have much to say about all of these Plutarchan principles of leadership save the last (the usefulness of a philosophy of Life and death). Most of Plutarch's heroes display all or most of the above characteristics. Some of Plutarch's heroes are remarkably deficient in one or two of these points. Intemperance, particularly with regard to improperly ordered affection toward money, sex, or celebrity destroyed several of the men whose lives he tells, notoriously the profligate Alcibiades, the befuddled Antony and the miserly Aristides. Lack of education limited the usefulness of Aristides native talents and was also the undoing of Marius. Plutarch specifically charges that had Crassus received a better education he might have been better equipped to shake off the avariciousness that so marred his character.

Excluding a few Lives which are incomplete (the first few inches of an ancient literary scroll being the most liable to damage) nearly every Life recounted by Plutarch yields telling anecdotes about the subject's childhood and youth. For Plutarch, the eminent men of ancient Greece and Rome became great leaders due, at least in part, to nature's gifts in the form of heredity, their childhood nurturing, and the education they received in their youth. In even a cursory reading of Plutarch, the presence, or absence, of the father emerges as a recurring theme.

A quick survey of the 46 parallel Lives of Plutarch reveals that better than a third of them had lost a parent (usually the father) when they were still children. Julius Caesar, Brutus who assassinated Caesar, Caesar's avenger Marc Anthony, and his successor Octavian Augustus Caesar all lost their fathers by the time they were in their early teens. Shall we assume that this singular fact is important for an understanding of the men whose lives Plutarch narrates? Plutarch apparently thought so—else why note it in so many of the Lives? Subsequent empirical analyses of the biographies of randomly selected groups of eminent men and women has confirmed the better than chance statistical association between loss of a parent in childhood and latter public eminence.

While no satisfactory explanation has yet been advanced to explain why losing a parent in childhood should help to produce later eminence, the relationship apparently is real. The modern literature confirms profound effects of father absence on children. For example, absence of a father is associated with earlier menarche in girls and higher levels of impulse control disorders in boys.

Education recurs as a theme in Plutarch's Lives. Interestingly, Plutarch does not rank birth (that is one parents), wealth, or location (coming from a famous city) nearly as highly as he places education when it comes to character formation. When Plutarch writes of Caius Marius, one of Rome's greatest military leaders and an inspiration for Julius Caesar, he tells us that Marius, for all his incomparable actions in battle, ultimately wrecked himself and ended his years in cruelty and vindictiveness because his passions had never been tamed by a liberal education.

Another example of the profound effects of education on destiny and character is Alexander the Great. Of Alexander's education what can we say, but that he had the finest available anywhere in the world in his time, or most any time? His teacher was Aristotle, perhaps the widest ranging thinker in human history.

Alexander was, Plutarch tells us, "naturally a great lover of all kinds of learning and reading." When campaigning, Alexander slept with a dagger and copy of Homer's *Iliad* under his pillow. He said that with these two tools close by he was prepared for come what may. Alexander was also a devoted reader of the great dramatists of the Hellenic world – Euripides, Sophocles, and Aeschylus– and other Greek authors.

From his reading, Alexander must have felt he had actually come to know his role models, Hercules, Achilles, and Cyrus the Great. The habits of the mind, developed in Alexander by his tutors and his reading, prepared him to seek the best models wherever they may be found.

An example of the effects of development of a philosophy for growth in leadership skills comes in the life of Cicero. Of Cicero, Plutarch tells us that he studied philosophy seriously and emerged as a synthesizer and popularizer of Greek learning. While he was not the most original thinker of the ancient world, he was one of the most influential as he summed up the accumulated centuries of philosophical and political thought and presented his summations in a compelling manner. In Athens he sought out voice teachers and instructors in the arts of rhetoric to train his voice and mind for public speaking. And as an advocate arguing cases in Rome he perfected the arts of persuasion. We will have more to say about Cicero in later chapters.

Virtually all of the Lives furnish us examples of the importance of ambition in producing good leaders. Virtually all of Plutarch's successful leaders evidenced a burning desire from early childhood to excel.

Plutarch relates of Cato the Younger, the implacable foe of Julius Caesar that when he was just 14 years old and seeing the heads of men said to be of great distinction brought thither, and observing the secret sighs of those that were present, he asked his preceptor, "Why does nobody kill this man?" "Because," said he, "they fear him, child, more than they hate him." "Why, then," replied Cato, "did you not give me a sword, that I might stab him, and free my country from this slavery?" (Life of Cato the Younger, 3)

Even as a youth, Julius Caesar was a threat to the tyrant Sylla, whom he fled only to be captured by pirates. When the pirates demanded 20 talents ransom, he laughed and told them they should have asked for more. The pirates then compound their mistakes about Caesar by thinking that he jests when, during his 38 days captivity, he says he'll have them all crucified. Sure enough after paying the ransom, he recruits some men to track the pirates down, captures them and, true to his word, has them all crucified.

Does modern scientific psychology back up these claims of Plutarch concerning the importance of early development in the life of the leader? What about Plutarch's emphasis on emulation and thinking 'big'? What about Plutarch's emphasis on use of rhetoric in leading men? What finally about his emphasis on the moral dimension of leadership? Is Plutarch correct about all of these elements of leadership? If so can an evolutionary approach illuminate any of the established relationships between them and later eminence and leadership?

We believe that the disciplines of evolutionary biology, biological anthropology and cognitive neurosciences can help provide new insights into these perplexing questions. In the following chapter, we will draw on these new scientific disciplines to focus on two questions; 1) the role of the leader in establishing and maintaining cooperation and 2) the evolutionary roots of charismatic leadership. A firm grounding in the literature on these two issues will stand us in good stead for much of the material that is to come in subsequent chapters.

Chapter 2

LEADERSHIP AND COOPERATION

In Chapter One we noted that the effects of particular early childhood events --presence or absence of the father, exposure to a liberal education, and early manifestations of leadership potential, were profound for later development of eminence and accomplishment. We also noted that classic biographers, such as Plutarch in his Lives, also noticed that these early childhood influences were a recurring theme among the great men he studied. Finally, we posited, again from Plutarch, four additional leadership traits that merit consideration in light of modern scientific findings. But before discussing these, we step back and consider the evolutionary origin and the societal purpose of leadership. In this chapter we lay out a framework for understanding the central role of the leader as one who, through prestige and dominance creates the conditions for order and cooperation in human societies.

Leaders create order out of chaos. Order and cooperation is central to human flourishing and the essence of good leadership. Just order involves and requires cooperation, and cooperation, we argue, does not arise spontaneously, but is called forth by the leader, that is by the good leader. Poor leaders create disorder. Thus, the key to a new theory of the phenomenon of leadership lies in the evolution and modes of cooperation in human societies.

New insights on cooperation have emerged from work in economics, cognitive neuroscience, and evolutionary psychology. Our reading of this emerging literature strongly suggests that the role of a leader is likely to be crucial in establishing and maintaining order and cooperation in human societies. You cannot get consistent cooperative behaviors from people in a group or enterprise unless there is a leader who gets the whole enterprise off the ground, who keeps the enterprise moving towards goals that all the members of the group endorse, who takes responsibility for insuring that 'free-riders' cannot exploit the cooperative group and who can protect the whole enterprise from dangers within and without the group.

Conversely a poor leader can create substantial disorder and chaos in a group or society. Consider the deleterious effects of unscrupulous leaders such as, Hitler, Stalin, Cromwell, Napoleon and dozens of other tyrants who hindered rather than advanced cooperation among ethnic groups and nations .The damage done by bad leaders demonstrates that wisely constituted law-governed or balanced or constitutional systems and republics can be rapidly and thoroughly subverted by scheming and unscrupulous individuals as long as those individuals command a constituency to support their subversive aims. This fragility of legal order underscores the importance, for good or bad, of the quality of leadership and the leaders who arise in any society.

The power of unscrupulous leaders to undermine cooperative enterprises and to sow chaos and bloodshed points to the importance of studying the relation of the leader to followers in order to truly understand the nature of leadership. Once again we will draw on the evolutionary and cognitive neurosciences to illuminate effects of leaders on their followers and on societies. We will also draw on a number of case studies of leader-follower relations taken from the ancient Greek historian, philosopher and biographer Plutarch, whom we introduced in the first chapter. But first let us summarize our argument for the centrality of leadership to cooperation and order.

EFFECTS OF 'GOOD' LEADERS

We contend that a good leader can create a just order out of chaos or an unjust order, or given an existing a legal order, sustain and promote and grow its best qualities. The historical evidence for these sorts of 'good' leaders is as abundant as the evidence for the catastrophic effects of 'bad' leaders on their societies. Hamilton, Madison (and Jay to some extent) not only formulated the philosophical, legal and institutional principles that underlay the operations of the nascent American republic, they actively brought that legal order to birth via their political activities. Similarly Solon in Athens and Lycurgus in Sparta brought legal order out of violent chaos for those two early Greek city states. To some extent religious founders such as Confucius, Moses, Jesus, Mohammed, and the Buddha can be understood as visionary leaders who brought new forms of cooperation and order to their societies. We will see in a later chapter how some forms of leadership are linked in their evolutionary roots to the emergence of ritual and religious forms of social cooperation. But first we wish to establish the link between leaders and the emergence of cooperation in social groups.

A 'good leader' protects against the effects of free-riders and thus creates conditions for successful cooperation. One of the fundamental impediments to establishment of any form of social cooperation is the problem of the 'free-rider'—the person who seeks to obtain the benefits of cooperation without paying any of the costs of cooperation. A free-rider lets everyone else do the work while he or she does nothing but collect the fruits of the work of others. No-one is willing to begin a cooperative enterprise if they believe that their work will be exploited by a free-rider. The corroding effects of the free-rider on social trust and cohesiveness therefore need to be controlled if cooperative groups are to get off the ground and flourish. How do human societies solve the problem of the free-rider?

The mathematical framework of game theory has been a central tool for understanding how cooperative entities can overcome the problem of the free-rider or the cheat. Game theory is also important for evolutionary theories of leadership and cooperation as it embodies the concept of *frequency dependent selection*. Frequency dependent selection refers to the fact that the success of any given behavioral strategy in a population of individuals will depend partially on the number of individuals who employ that strategy. Cooperative behavioral strategies will be successful to the extent that most of the population buys into them. Since people will only cooperate with others who can be trusted to do their fair share of the work, human societies have developed ways to identify and neutralize the corrosive effects of these free-riders. Our claim will be that one solution to the problem of the free rider was the development of the 'leader'.

THE PRISONER'S DILEMMA (PD)

To see how the leader can solve the problem of the free rider we invoke the classical problem from game theory known as the prisoner's dilemma (PD). First some background on the history of the intersection between game theory and evolutionary biology. Maynard Smith and Price (1973) and Trivers (1971) launched the modern study of cooperative behavioral strategies in human populations by marrying evolutionary biology with the mathematical rigor of game theory. Trivers' concept of reciprocal altruism ('I scratch your back if you scratch mine') was tested with game theory simulations by Axelrod and Hamilton in 1981 (discussed in Axelrod, 1984). Their simulations were based on the Prisoner's Dilemma game (PD), perhaps the single most famous metaphor for the problem of cooperation in human societies. In this game, two guilty prisoners are interrogated by a policeman in separate rooms. If neither of them talks they both go free. If one of them blames the other then the other will go to jail. Thus, 'not talking' depends on how much trust exists between the 2 prisoners. The dilemma comes from the fact that if both of them keeps their mouths shut they go free—yet neither of them can afford to do so because they need to accuse the other to go free themselves. If they do not accuse the other they risk being the sole person accused of the crime. If both prisoners talk (accuse the other) they both go to jail! If only one talks the other goes to jail. If neither talk, i.e. if they succeed in trusting one another, they both go free. Thus the problem is one of trust. Cooperation in the PD cannot get off the ground unless trust can be established.

To put the PD in a slightly more quantitative form, when both prisoners talk (defect), the mean population payoff is lower than if both had cooperated—had trusted one another not to talk. Players in the PD (the prisoners in this case) can adopt either one of two strategies: cooperate (C) or defect (D). Cooperation in the PD means to trust and NOT talk. Cooperation, since it is risky, results in a benefit b to the opposing player, but incurs a cost c to the cooperator (where $b > c > 0$); defection has no costs or benefits. Whether the opponent plays C or D, it is, therefore, better to play D.

The PD embodies the problem of cooperation: although individuals can benefit from mutual cooperation, they can do even better by exploiting the trust and cooperation of others. The prisoner who defects and accuses his partner when the partner keeps his mouth shut…gets the highest possible payoff, he goes free and gets all the loot. This guy is the 'free-rider'.

How do you deal with this unsavory character? One way might be to become better able to identify the untrustworthy betrayers (free-riders). Perhaps they behave a certain way. Yet, they may behave charmingly, and seduce you into cooperating with them all the while they are lying to your face. In order therefore to detect a potential free-rider you need to learn how to detect liars. But exhaustive studies of liar detection abilities of humans show that people perform only at chance levels in detecting lies and deceit (Vrij, 2004). In evolutionary terms every time a population of individuals became good at detecting these liars, the liars became better at concealing their lies…Hence there is a never-ending arms race between the free-riding liars and the cooperators. In short trying to a priori identify who is going to lie to you won't work as a solution to the free rider problem.

REPUTATION AND THE RISE OF THE LEADER

Another solution depends on 'reputation'. If you could remember who failed to cooperate in the past or who lied to you in the past then you could avoid that person in the future. If you then told others about that person then that person would develop a reputation as a liar. That poor reputation would then protect the cooperators against the free-riders. This may be called application of the 'once bitten twice shy' rule. In the 'Iterated Prisoner's Dilemma (IPD)', a single game consists of a number of rounds of the simple PD, which allows individuals to react to an opponent's past behavior. If players interact repeatedly before the final tally is made, free-riders will learn to expect low payoffs in future interactions because of retaliation by the people they betrayed. Thus, game theory simulations support the view that reputation can affect behavioral strategies. In the context of the social group in the real world the free-riders' poor reputation limits their abilities to cheat and thus increases the abilities of the rest of the social group to cooperate. Good reputations also played a role. If you developed a reputation for being trustworthy, talented or beneficial to cooperate with more resources in the form of social alliances would flow your way. Thus, avoiding a bad reputation and cultivating a good reputation was key to success among early human groups. This 'reputation' solution appears to be one piece of the overall solution to the problem of cooperation adopted by human beings. It was also the first step in the development of the leader.

Now consider what happens to an individual branded a free-rider by someone he betrayed in a previous cooperative enterprise. That person would now have a reputation as a free-rider and thus no-one would agree to cooperate with him and his 'fitness' (access to reproductive and resource opportunities etc) would be drastically curtailed and thus free-riders would, at least theoretically, be eliminated from the population. But as we all knew free-riders have not been eliminated from the human population. So the reputation solution is not a fully adequate solution. Something more was needed.

CHARACTER MATTERS

Attempting to identify and remember who the free-riders are does not appear, by itself, to be a wholly satisfactory solution to the free –rider problem. If however it is paired with its converse, the development of memory and information about individuals who are NOT free-riders, i.e. individuals who are trustworthy and honest, then the role of reputation becomes doubly important for cooperation. In short, if we developed a good memory for two types of persons, the free-riders and the trustworthy ones then we become doubly able to promote cooperation…by limiting our losses from exploitation by free-riders and by increasing our successes via identification of trustworthy persons. In such a society (where everyone had excellent memories for who the bad guys and the good guys were) a poor reputation could kill you. It would certainly limit the ability of free-riders to exploit cooperators in that society. Conversely, the development of a good reputation would enhance your status considerably and put you in an influential and leadership role in the society. A good reputation would, furthermore, allow cooperators to find one another and to form relationships of trust with one another, thus considerably advancing the cause of order and cooperation in the society.

Yet, there is still a fly in the ointment here. How do we know when we are dealing with an honest cooperator or with a lying free –rider? Reputations are not always reliable indicators of past behavior. Who are we to believe when one person claims that another betrayed and exploited him in some past cooperative endeavor? The accuser or the accused? Conversely, how do we tell when a person is really an honest and trustworthy cooperator? Certainly obtaining information about the person in question from as many sources as possible (i.e., gossip) would help but the quality of the information obtained from gossip is always suspect given that envy, hatred and competition could influence talk about others.

In order to fairly and adequately evaluate the 'reputation' of an individual we would have to get to know the person over time. We would have to add up all of the social interactions we have had with that person and perhaps collect testimonies from other people who interacted with him in the past. Only information derived from repeated interactions with an individual can yield reliable information about the enduring qualities of that individual. Therefore, we would need to remember not only people's reputations but we would also have to remember our past interactions with everyone that we might form a cooperative enterprise with. Thus the problem of the free-rider has, to some extent, driven the evolution of memory capacity and intelligence.

In short, it is through observation and memory of repeated interactions that we collect information on the person's *character and trustworthiness*. We seek a collaborator who is trustworthy, reliable, smart, and worth forming a cooperative partnership with. We obtain the necessary background information on candidates by listening to gossip around *character*. Therefore we may affirm that the *content of character* is vitally important for the emergence of human cooperation because it is knowledge of character that helps solve the problem of the free-rider. While a free-rider may be able to lie his way into a partnership he would never be able to sustain over time the virtues associated with development of a sterling character. It is simply too costly for someone like a free-rider to develop a reliable, trustworthy, honest character. Indeed development of integrity of character is difficult for all of us and that is why development of character is so valuable a 'method' for promoting cooperation.

Character is a reliable index to a person's willingness and ability to cooperate. *In early human societies we hypothesize that the best characters, those with the optimal combination of trustworthiness, wisdom, intelligence, integrity become leaders.* This does not mean that there were no poor or murderous leaders among early humans-merely that there was an evolutionary dynamic that favored, but did not ensure, the development of valorizing what we would now call character strengths like wisdom, intelligence and integrity. The evolutionary dynamic was strong enough that it produced some individuals who apparently were talented leaders and who were individuals of sterling character.

So one evolutionary source of leadership is the value placed on character and reputation by early human groups. This was one way that these early human groups promoted cooperation. In a later chapter we will link this emphasis on character and reputation with the phenomenon of 'prestige' to explain what we believe is one of the two major leadership styles that occur in human societies. To forecast these styles: one is prestige oriented and depends on reputation, character and accomplishment. The other major style is what we have called 'dominance'. The emphasis with the dominance strategy is on force and coercion of others. While non-violent political and legal tools can be used to enact a dominance strategy, violent coercion is the fundamental back-up for the dominance strategy. Nevertheless, under normal circumstances force need not be employed by a leader who can effectively utilize political and legal tools at his disposal. We will later claim that really effective leadership uses both strategies to accomplish all the tasks a leader must accomplish and that context determines which strategy is 'best'.

From an evolutionary theoretical point of view 'character' functions as a signal to others. In effect it says to others:

> "I possess a sterling character …therefore you can trust me for purposes of cooperation. I will contribute more than my fair share and will not betray you. You can believe these claims because 'character' cannot be faked by the free-riders."

In evolutionary psychology these kinds of hard-to-fake signals are called costly signals. It will be worth discussing the functions of costly signaling in human communication and human societies as costly signaling is crucial for understanding diverse leadership behaviors.

ROOTS OF LEADERSHIP IN COSTLY SIGNALS AND RITUAL

Recall that our consideration of potential solutions to the free-rider problem foundered on the issue of reputation. While branding free-riders with a bad reputation will help protect cooperators against exploitation, it is obvious that reputations can be faked. Intentions in general to cooperate or defect (free-ride) can be hidden and faked. An individual can improve his poor reputation by behaving like a cooperator…e.g., by helping fellows in need.

Actually helping others in need of course is a costly behavior that most free-riders would likely try to avoid. Thus, this helping behavior can be considered an honest indicator of a person's willingness to cooperate. Similar costly helping behaviors would correspondingly enhance a person's good reputation. In fact it turns out that the more costly the behaviors the greater the trustworthiness of the signal. If someone helps an old lady across the street that is one thing but if someone sells all he has and gives to the poor that is quite another. Our certainty that the latter person is serious about his desire to cooperate is enhanced by the very costliness of the altruistic behavior he emits. The impact of these sorts of costly behaviors on cooperation in a group is very clearly seen in the context of a religious group.

How can members of a religious group tell that a new member is sincere and thereby deserves all the benefits of the group? If the person in question merely attends worship services once a week then that is one thing…but if in addition, he is seen praying frequently, wearing religious signs, uniforms, and other external 'badges', if he contributes time and services to the groups' programs and coffers and so on then group members' confidence in the sincerity of that individual correspondingly increases. In general the costlier the behavior the more trustworthy the claims are of the person emitting those behaviors.

COSTLY SIGNALING THEORY

The latter considerations are summed up in so-called costly signaling theory. Costly signaling theory first emerged in the context of sexual selection. Sexual selection theory suggests that some traits may have evolved because they signal fitness of the bearer. If, for example, the trait in question is facial symmetry, a feature apparently correlated with attractiveness ratings in humans, then sexual selection theory would predict that the trait "facial symmetry" would likely be correlated with some fitness-enhancing gene such as a disease-resistant gene. Potential mates will then favor reproductive partners who display facial symmetry, and thus the trait "facial symmetry" will increase in the population. Other traits such as large antlers might indicate the presence of parasite-resistance genes in a reindeer or elk. Large antlers will, in effect, advertise presence of these "good genes." This, in turn, creates selective pressures for displaying and enhancing such advertisements. Males without the parasite-resistant gene will not be able to display large antlers, as they will not be able to metabolically grow and maintain the antlers without paying a metabolic cost that in turn will make them more vulnerable to parasite infestation. Thus large antlers, although costly to produce and thus an expensive handicap, will nevertheless constitute an honest signal of good genes, and thus honest communication between potential mates will be possible. In short, costly signaling makes communication possible under adverse conditions; that is, conditions in which the parties have partially conflicting interests.

According to costly signaling theory, a signal is defined as a behavior, expression, or phenotype produced by one individual (the signaler) that aims to influence the behavior of a second individual (the receiver). Under conditions of conflict, the two parties may be motivated to transmit nonveridical, deceptive information in order to obtain an advantage. If one individual can gain an advantage from another by concealing information or by sending misleading information, he or she will do so. In the short run, at least, using deception would sometimes seem to have advantages.

But fundamentally, communication must require that signals be honest and reliable, at least on average. If they were not reliable, the intended receivers would evolve to ignore them. Costly signals appear to have evolved in order to guarantee the reliability and honesty of a communication system. Communication will be stable when the signaler and receiver pursue strategies that together comprise a signaling equilibrium such that neither party gains from unilateral defection to deception or change in strategy. To keep both signaler and receiver in the game, hard-to-fake signals must be utilized.

Grafen (1990) modeled the evolution of a courtship signaling handicap strategy as a "continuous asymmetric scramble game" wherein females have the upper hand (they are the choosier sex) and are thus in a position to choose male partners based on their apparent quality. In Grafen's formal model, males vary continuously (from low-quality to high-quality males) in the qualities females wish to assess. Both females and high-quality males seek to find a way for males to honestly display their qualities and to prevent low-quality males from mimicking high-quality males. Males also vary continuously in at least one feature of interest to females. It may, for example, be intensity of song or dance. Thus, males choosing not to vary their displays (strategy 1) in terms of intensity relative to their quality (i.e., choosing to adopt an uninformative strategy with respect to female observers) will be matched against males who choose to let display intensity vary with quality (strategy 2).

Females, for their part, also adopt two fundamentally different strategies: Some females may choose a skeptical stance, treating all display intensities as the same. Others will use intensity information to rank the males in terms of quality and to make choices regarding mating partners. Male fitness in the model therefore depends on a male's inherent quality, the costs of putting on the display, and the degree to which females use display intensity to rank and choose male partners. The ranking procedure females use defines this game as a scramble competition, as it forces males to compete against other males. The payoff for any one male depends on how well other males perform. Female fitness in the model is maximal when female rankings of male quality are accurate or close to true male quality. Clearly, female fitness rises in proportion to the quality of her choices.

Grafen (1990) showed that this game has two equilibrium points or evolutionary stable strategies (strategies resistant to invasion by other strategies): (1) Males do not display honestly and females ignore all displays, and (2) all or most males are honest and all or most females choose according to display intensity. The second evolutionary stable strategy occurs only if four conditions are met: (1) The higher the perceived quality of a male, the more likely a female will choose him (quality *is* what the females are using to make their choices); (2) signaling must be costly for males, which obtains because a male's fitness decreases while he is performing the display (because all performances require some effort); (3) effort invested in the display/performance must cost less for a high-quality male (he has resources to spare) than for a low-quality male; and (4) both low- and high-quality males receive the same payoffs if they are (due to error) given the same quality ranking by a female.

The condition ensuring signal honesty is number 3 (lower costs incurred by higher-quality males). The payoff to males depends on display intensity, and thus males have an incentive to increase intensity of their displays. This incentive, however, could lead to an arms race in which each male attempts to increase intensity relative to every other male. Thus, every male would be obliged to pay higher and higher display/performance costs to stay in the race. Eventually, costs would exceed benefits of engaging in the scramble competition and this break-even point would occur at a lower total cost for low-quality males than for high-quality males. In short, Grafen showed that costly signaling can be an evolutionary stable strategy under conditions where a skeptical receiver and a potentially deceptive sender must communicate. Such conditions, of course, are almost universal among animals and humans, and thus the application of the costly-signaling paradigm is expected to be extensive.

Grafen's results do not mean that communication systems must employ costly signals in order to ensure honesty, only that employment of costly signals can work to stabilize a communication system if the parties exchanging signals choose to employ costly signals. That choice is more likely under conditions of escalating conflict where arms races might occur, to the mutual ruin of all parties.

Our contention is that character can be seen as a costly signal that functions to stabilize human groups considering cooperating. Given the inherent difficulty (costliness) in forming a character of consistent honesty, reliability, integrity, self-sacrifice, trustworthiness and intelligence, 'sterling character' was rare in early human societies. When it appeared that person would take on leadership roles in the group the character of the person likely came under intense scrutiny. To become a leader in early human societies therefore required that you have a trustworthy and indeed a sterling reputation and character. The followers could use the information derived from scrutiny of your character and reputation to satisfy themselves that you the leader would not exploit them. Nevertheless, they still needed some help in protecting them from other potential free-riders in the group.

A sterling character in the leader was not sufficient to deal with the problem of the free-riders in the group. While trustworthy characters allowed individuals to identify the cooperators with good reliability, it did not eliminate free-riders. Something else was needed to minimize the tendency to free-ride on the work of others. That next ingredient was the development of a process of punishment of the free-riders.

LEADERS PUNISH FREE–RIDERS AND ENFORCE THE LAWS

In the classical prisoner dilemma, cooperation is all or nothing, since this game has only two strategies (defect or cooperate). However, in the real world the cooperation of individuals can vary continuously, sometimes being conditional on previous moves of an opponent or on the reputation of an opponent and so forth. In the real world most cooperative enterprises usually involve more than one other 'player'. How might evolutionary game theory handle strategic and cooperative interactions among a small group of individuals? The generalization of PD type interactions to groups of arbitrary size N is known as 'Public Goods' games (Kagel and Roth, 1995). In a typical Public Goods experiment a group of, e.g. six players gets an endowment of $10 each. Every player then has the option to invest part or all of their money into a common pool knowing that the experimenter is going to triple the amount in the pool and divide it equally among all players regardless of their contribution. If everybody invests their money, each player ends up with $30. However, each invested dollar only yields a return of 50 cents to the investor. Therefore, if everybody plays rationally, no one will invest, and hence the group of players will forego the benefits of the public good. In formal terms and assuming that players either defect or fully cooperate, the payoff for defectors becomes Pd ¼ a nc c/N, while the payoff for cooperators is Pc ¼ Pd) c, where a is the multiplication factor of the common pool, nc the number of cooperators in the group, and c is the cost of the cooperative investment. As in the PD, defection dominates and cooperators are doomed (Hauert and Szabó, 2003). Larger Public Goods groups correspond to larger numbers of single PD interactions. This implies that defectors can exploit cooperators more efficiently in larger groups, and hence that cooperation becomes increasingly difficult to achieve as social group size increases, which remains true even if interactions are iterated (Boyd and Richerson, 1988; Hauert and Schuster, 1998; Matsushima and Ikegami, 1998).

Interestingly, in experimental Public Goods games human subjects *do not follow the best or most rational strategy (i.e., the free-rider strategy* with the largest payoff). Instead people, at least initially in the opening moves of the game opt to share their money and to cooperate. Because, this sort of 'irrational' cooperative behavior undermines rationality assumptions in economics (Fehr and Gachter 2002), theorists have had to ask: 'Why do people opt for a cooperative strategy in the opening gambit of a public goods game?' As in the case of the iterated prisoners dilemma answers to this question likely involve issues related to reward, punishment and reputation (Milinski et al., 2002).

We discussed the role of reputation and character above. It is now time to discuss the role of punishment in the evolution of cooperation in human societies. Punishment is common in nature (Clutton-Brock and Parker, 1995), ranging from the aggressive displays of the dominant alpha male in gorilla societies to institutionalized civil and criminal law in humans. The success of cooperators hinges on the ability to condition cooperation on information about the opponent's reputation, i.e. about whether the opponent punishes defection, and to adjust the behavior accordingly (Brandt et al., 2003; Hauert et al., 2004; Sigmund et al., 2001). These sorts of conditional social interactions occur in two stages: first individuals decide whether to cooperate or to defect; second, individuals may punish the opponent, conditioned on the outcome of the first stage. This 2-part process results in four basic behavioral types in these games of cooperation: 1) the social strategy G1 that cooperates and punishes defection, 2) the paradoxical strategy G2 that defects but punishes, 3) the asocial G3 strategy that neither cooperates nor punishes, and finally 4) the mild G4 strategy that cooperates but does not punish. G2 (defects and punishes) is paradoxical because it does poorly when facing other G2 players. The asocial G3 strategy (neither cooperates or punishes) may actually do well for a while (eventually reaches 'fixation' in the language of biology) because it is left alone by opponents. The G4 (cooperate) strategy can increase in numbers through random drift and thereby unwittingly facilitate successful invasions by the asocial G3 strategists. Thus if you cooperate without punishing the asocial people the asocial people will increase in number and no cooperation in the group will emerge.

This outcome changes dramatically if both punishment and reputation is introduced, i.e. if individuals may learn about the punishing inclinations of their opponent. In short, if potential cooperators observe that exploitation by free-riders is punished then they are more likely to cooperate.

In early human societies it is likely that punishment had to be done by an individual who possessed both political support and brute physical strength. The combination of political and physical strength can be understood as the adoption of a 2-fold strategy by leaders in early human groups: that of reputation/prestige and of political 'dominance'. Prestige-oriented strategies relied on reputation and character to elicit trust in others. Political dominance relied on punishment of free-riders to elicit cooperation in others.

We contend that the leader in early human societies had this capacity to use their reputation and prestige as well as their political dominance to promote group cooperation and social order. In the pure case dominance needs no lengthy analysis: the leader who relies exclusively on dominance simply uses force (either legal or military) to keep followers and opponents in line. It may be a serviceable tool for leadership for a time, but cannot be maintained without the support of prestige.

In the coming chapters we will examine some theories of the evolutionary origins of prestige in human societies. We shall also return to our ancient guide Plutarch for specific examples and lessons from the lives of men who impressed both their own and our age with their leadership abilities. We will see how this 2-part strategic approach to leadership played out in the lives of leaders from the classical age. It is relatively easy to understand how dominance leads to success for the leader. He simply uses force (either legal or military) to keep followers and opponents in line. The prestige strategy we contend is equally powerful. Indeed dominance without prestige will not work for long. It is necessary to combine the two strategies for any human cooperative enterprise to flourish. In order to see the power of the prestige strategy it will be necessary to elucidate in the next several chapters a couple of the other functions of the leader.

Chapter 3

DYNAMICS OF LEADER-FOLLOWER RELATIONS

INTRODUCTION

We have seen how both prestige and political dominance including the ability to punish free-riders was essential to early leaders. We have also seen that costly signals or traits were essential attributes of the leader. The very costliness of the trait meant that it was hard to fake and therefore reliable as a signal of quality of the individual possessing the trait. Followers could therefore both identify potential leaders on the basis of these costly signals (e.g., strong character traits) and trust such individuals as leaders. We also probed the origins of these traits in individual leaders in their native drive to do great things and with reference to early influences from family and education. Now we may turn to our fourth leadership trait, one of particular importance to the prestige-based leadership mode –emulation of a worthy individual.

Recent advances in the study of leadership have led to renewed interest in the leader-follower relation as key to understanding leadership dynamics and change (Antonakis and Atwater, 2002; Bass, 1998; Burns, 1978; Greenleaf, 1996; Lee, 1993). We too emphasize the centrality of the follower to an understanding of the nature of leadership. Our interest is theoretically motivated. As we have seen in the introductory chapter, human cooperation is not possible without a group of individuals who coalesce around a leader whose reputation for intelligence, energy and trustworthiness fit them for leadership roles in any given cooperative enterprise.

We argue that for cooperation to succeed followers have to become, over time, leaders, and thus that one primary task of a leader is to turn followers into leaders. A poor leader will attempt to induce fear, passivity and blind obedience in his followers while a positive leader will do the opposite: dispel fears, educate followers and push followers into taking responsibility for leadership. How then does a positive leader turn followers into leaders?

We contend that one path whereby close followers become leaders is via "emulation" or imitation of the character and skills of the leader. It is easy to underestimate the power of these processes of imitation and emulation in the transformation of followers into leaders, as much of emulation is unconscious and even involuntary. Advances in the cognitive neurosciences (reviewed below) have revealed that imitation can be either conscious or unconscious but is most often unconscious and compulsive. It occurs in virtually all social interactions, and is, finally, one of the most powerful learning mechanisms human beings possess.

The automatic nature of the imitation process and the efficiency with which it facilitates acquisition of new behaviors and skills is both a blessing and a curse for us...a blessing, because it is effortless and therefore a powerful inculturation and learning tool; a curse because it is non-discriminatory in what it learns. If the imitator is exposed only to negative models then his/her behavior rapidly comes to resemble the negative models. To the extent that imitative learning is unconscious it largely controls our behaviors and goals. When emulation is uncritical and unconscious, negative character traits and behaviors are more likely to be acquired. All too often this is the case when the leader is perceived as charismatic and distant (Conger, 1998).

The power and ubiquity of imitative learning suggests that it will be crucial in understanding both positive and negative forms of the leader-follower social relationship. In particular, it will be important in understanding how followers acquire the leadership skills and traits of their leaders and, therefore, we focus on this issue (how emulation facilitates the transformation of followers into leaders) in this chapter.

Emulation of character traits and skills of the leader as a path to eminence and power was ubiquitous and fascinating to the ancient philosophers, among them Plutarch. The idea explained why great men tended to appear together in history. Why, after all, was it the case that when Caesar appeared you also found Cato, Pompey, Cicero, and others of similar political ability? Why, when Socrates appeared, did you also find him bracketed in one or two generations before by Anaxagoras and after by Plato and Aristotle, and others of similar philosophic ability? The Roman historian Vellius Paterculas suggested that

> "Genius is fostered by emulation, and it is now envy, now admiration, which enkindles imitation, and in the nature of things, that which is cultivated with the highest zeal advances to the highest perfection; but it is difficult to continue at the point of perfection, and naturally that which cannot advance must recede. And as in the beginning we are fired with the ambition to overtake those whom we regard as leaders, so when we have despaired of being able either to surpass or even to equal them, our zeal wanes with our hope; it ceases to follow what it cannot overtake, and abandoning the old field as though pre-empted, it seeks a new one."[1]

Vellius explicitly notes that genius is attained via emulation. He points out that clusters of men of genius in some field of endeavor arise when one individual sets a level of accomplishment and then others, impressed by that accomplishment, or envious of it, seek to imitate it. Those who are merely envious will never attain to true emulation and so will fail in the quest to match the model's greatness. For those who emulate the model out of admiration, chances are better. To greater or lesser degrees these imitators rise to the challenge of the master. They make new contributions, some of which match or surpass that of the master. In doing so, they, in turn, elicit new imitators as they rise to eminence. Like the original master/model they then foster growth of those who admire them. When they cannot equal or surpass the master/model in accomplishment they abandon the field and seek out new opportunities or give up altogether.

---

[1] The above quote was taken from Dean Simonton's text on "Greatness" (1994, p. 377-378) who, in turn, had taken it from Kroeber's studies on 'Configurations of Culture Growth' (1944)

Emulation will not always work to pull you up into leadership. Where there are already many great leaders in a field it becomes very difficult to equal or to surpass the accomplishments of the masters. So the new contributions in an old field of endeavor no longer work as well as they once did to make the reputation of new leaders. In such a situation the stream of outstanding leaders in that field of endeavor begin to diminish and aspirants cease to enter it. The 'bar' has been set too high for the current generation of aspirants. They will need to wait for new technical discoveries or new insights to emerge before someone can surpass the work and accomplishments of the field's current master/model. If aspirants can no longer match the model, if for example, no one can match Cato's or Cicero's vigorous defense of the Republic, then articulate and politically savvy defenders of the republic will no longer appear. If no sculptor can hope to equal or surpass Michelangelo's David, then artistic aspirants will find models in some other field of endeavor.

According to Plutarch, admiration at the emotional level is antagonistic to envy. One cannot attain to greatness via envy. Envy is inimical to true emulation and therefore inimical to acquisition of excellence or nobility of character. When you are envious of your model, of a great man or woman, you inevitably cultivate feelings of anger, resentment and hatred and thus you will find it difficult to admire or like the great leader you are attempting to imitate. If you do not like him/her you will find it difficult to see things from his perspective, to put on 'his Mind" and to walk in his shoes etc. In short, you will fail in your project of emulation. Your feelings of resentment and envy will convince you of the lie that you are not capable of becoming a great leader. Envy assumes that you lack something while emulation assumes that you have the capacity to acquire what your model has…that the project of emulation will be successful.

When you emulate a worthy model, a great man, out of admiration for his virtues, accomplishments and his character, then you *will be* able to empathize with him, you will be able to take his point of view on things, you will be able to 'walk in his shoes' and so on. Thus the key to acquiring the man's greatness or skill is to consciously focus on imitating the man's character and virtues as you can naturally admire these excellences. The project to become like him will then work. Your admiration will short-circuit passivity and envy-the twin dangers involved in being a follower.

The follower-related dangers of envy and passivity should therefore occupy some of the energies of a good leader. A leader of excellence will develop techniques for forestalling envy and passivity among his or her followers. Plutarch presents numerous instances in his Lives of otherwise excellent leaders failing to deal with the envy of followers –especially close followers and this failure leading to the leader's downfall. Brutus' assassination of Caesar, the Athenians' exile of Alcibiades, Crassus' envy of Pompey and Caesar sent him on the foolhardy expedition into Persia and so on. Envy destroys human beings, both followers and leaders. Plutarch would say that this is because it prevents a person from emulating true virtues and thus to grow into wisdom and leadership. A good leader will expect to become the target of other people's envy and then will prepare to defuse it by providing opportunities for followers to grow into leadership responsibilities.

Good leaders are all around us if we would but search them out. Dean Simonton, a scholar in the field of creativity and leadership studies who underscored the role of emulation in achievement of greatness, noted that effective emulation can be of two kinds, emulation of someone present or emulation of someone absent but vividly brought to memory:

"Emulation is a social psychological process ...entailing one person's becoming enthralled by the accomplishments of another person... We must acknowledge that imitation follows two routes. First those who aspire to greatness can admire and ape the achievements of predecessors at a distance, without personal contact. Indeed these idols may no longer walk among the living. Second, aspirants can interact in a more intimate capacity of disciples, apprentices, or pupils. Predecessors who influence development indirectly we may loosely style 'models'; those who act directly we can call "mentors" (Simonton, 1994, p. 378).

Clearly, when we read Plutarch's 'Lives' we are learning from models who are no longer 'among the living'. Plutarch gives us such a variety of examples, personalities, circumstances, characters, events and conditions that his models cannot fail to conduce to the most thoroughgoing education in the art of emulating a noble character or a worthy model of leadership. Perhaps that is why Plutarch's Lives has functioned as a sort of manual for aspiring leaders on leadership and eminence from the ancient world to the modern era.

Our focus on Plutarch and on emulation of the best of virtues of the best of the leaders underscores the crucial importance of biography in leadership studies. The greater the exposure to good models in 'real life' and in biographies, the better the chances for growth in leadership character traits and skills.

One needs, then, to imitate a worthy and admirable leader if you are to become a worthy and effective leader. The fire of leadership can only be kindled in the heart, Plutarch claims, when we are exposed to the influence of great and admirable leaders. The way to achieve leadership and then greatness is to emulate the virtues, boldness and excellences of great leaders and the only way to emulate them effectively is to get to know them. The best way to get to know them is to study and admire them. If we do not admire them then we will not like them. If we do not like them we will fail in our desire to imitate them. Thus, it is crucial to elicit admiration in the emulator/ reader.

In order to increase our ability to admire his subjects and to decrease the chances that we will dislike them or merely envy them, Plutarch always focused on describing the moral character of the leaders he studied. His method of describing parallel lives helped him to bring into vivid relief the impact of character on leadership quality or indeed on fate of the individuals and societies involved. With the comparative method he shows us two comparable men facing comparable leadership challenges –yet under slightly different conditions and given slightly different characters. When the reader is tempted to condemn the man under consideration, there is Plutarch already pointing out the character flaw while noting later that a comparable figure faced similar circumstances and showed less courage than the man under consideration and so forth. Plutarch consistently finds ways to help us put on the Mind of the man in question, to 'walk in his shoes', to set aside arbitrary judgment, while yet, inciting intense admiration of the noble qualities of the man himself.

Plutarch has shown that the way to elicit admiration, and to excite leadership stirrings in the reader, the reader must be exposed to the leader's moral and political character, his wiliness and strategic sense, his political daring and audacity, his recklessness and passions, his political dreams and desire to dominate, his accomplishments and his moral failing in order to excite in us equivalent leadership virtues.

Because Plutarch wanted to activate the reader's ability to admire nobility of spirit and to inhibit petty feelings of envy and defeatism that could forestall leadership potential, he labored to depict how 'character' determined destiny and virtue—'virtue' in the ancient sense of the term as an 'excellence' or a 'nobility'. There is a grandeur in the display of excellence of character, in particular, according to Plutarch. One of its primary properties according to Plutarch is that great characters inspire emulation. In the famous passage (partially quoted above) from the life of Pericles, Plutarch notes that there are many things and people that we admire but do not seek to imitate or emulate. We may be taken with the talents of an artist or an artisan but we do not attempt to emulate the artist. The fact that we admire a statue by Phidias does not mean that we admire Phidias himself. But the drama of a character, who in adversity or in prosperity reveals hidden strengths and a nobility of spirit that issues in virtuous and bold action is different. Such a display of spirit, Plutarch wrote, can so affect men's minds as to create at once both admiration of the things done and a desire to imitate the person who accomplishes such deeds.

For Plutarch then what elicits the capacity to emulate and therefore to become a great leader is to witness nobility of character. But we need to see such a spirit in action to realize that we have the same spirit within us as well and that we too can become a leader. Emulation of a worthy model therefore lies at the heart of the Plutarchan prescription for eminence and leadership.

The Science of Emulation

Can we trust Plutarch's contention that emulation is a reliable path to leadership? Imitation is one of the most powerful learning methods we possess. We were designed to learn via imitation. Learning via imitation is written into our brain and cells. In what follows, we will present evidence from the latest findings in the cognitive and brain sciences which supports the claim that the strongest and most reliable way to learn new behavioral repertoires is to imitate a person who displays those skills. First, we want to review recent evidence from empirical studies of correlates of greatness/eminence. When researchers search for causes of greatness and accomplishment by studying the lives of thousands of leaders, artists, scientists, generals and so forth, the best predictors of greatness and accomplishment turn out be hard work, persistence, and most importantly for us: the existence of models to emulate.

Simonton (1994; 1995; 1999), for example, marshaled a huge amount of historical evidence that supports the idea that emulation of a worthy model can lead to eminence or greatness. He looked at what personality, behavioral and environmental factors were associated with eminence and accomplishment in the arts and sciences across 2500 years of history. His database consisted of about 5000 creative persons in Western civilization who lived from 700 BC to AD 1839, and aggregated into 'generations' consisting of about twenty years apiece. After sifting through a variety of potential predictors of eminence and creativity from personality characteristics, to social and environmental conditions, Simonton found *that the strongest predictor of creativity in a current generation of leaders was the number of creative persons and products in the two preceding generations!* In other words, leaders in the arts and sciences tend to appear in clusters in the space of two to three generations and then disappear. If you considered any one of these creative individuals and asked what factors best predicted his or her appearance on the scene and his accomplishments, those factors were *not* family background, schooling, economic conditions, political climate, or even health characteristics. Instead the strongest predictors were the appearance one or two generations back, of someone who achieved eminence in the relevant field and to whom the creator looked for inspiration.

As Simonton himself suggested his data strongly imply that creation of a cluster of 'greats' in any field of endeavor occurs when you have models of leadership with which to work toward and against. The leaders themselves testify to this fact when they say in their autobiographies that they strived to respond to the stimulus provided by their predecessors. The 'imitation effect' is not confined to just western leaders either. Simonton found similar results in an analysis of 10,000 Chinese leaders during a similar span of time (840 BC to AD 1979). More recently. Charles Murray, in his massively researched work on "Human Accomplishment" (Murray, 2003) has replicated Simonton's results with an even larger database than that of Simonton. Murray not only added hundreds of other creative individuals to Simonton's database he also looked at men and women of eminence across cultures and cultural epochs. His databases included individuals from the Western, Chinese, Arabic, Indian and other civilizations. Murray once again found that one of the top predictors of accomplishment in any given field was the existence of models in the current or previous generation. Murray, furthermore, exhaustively investigated all kinds of alternative explanations for the appearance of leaders to that of emulation but nevertheless largely confirmed Simonton's previous findings. The best predictors of leadership, creativity and eminence turn out to be the availability of 'models'-as we defined them above. These data strongly suggest that the most reliable path to leadership and eminence is, as Plutarch believed, emulation of a worthy model.

Given that emulation may play a role in acquisition of key skills of leadership, how concretely does it do so?

Here we turn to the evolutionary and cognitive neurosciences for answers. First we note that imitation is pervasive in human behavior. We are very good at mirroring the people we are exposed to, so good that sometimes it feels as if it is involuntary. Emulation is, in fact, one of the fundamental mechanisms of learning. We learn how to interact with others by watching our parents. We learn how to learn by watching a teacher. We learn the principles of a craft through apprenticeship. We learn fine motor skills by imitating the pattern of motor sequences exhibited by the expert and so on. The brain, in fact, exhibits an astonishing degree of plasticity such that it is capable of re-producing virtually anything it imitates and when it does so repeatedly that brain or person has learnt or acquired the behaviors it once simply imitated.

When you consistently imitate a model you eventually incorporate that model's behavioral repertoire into your own behavioral repertoire. To back up this last claim we first summarize the evolution of imitative learning and then we turn to the neurology of imitative learning. At the end of this walk-through of the details of the science of emulation it will be clear that emulation of the skills and character of exceptional people is indeed the most effective route to acquiring those same skills.

EVOLUTION OF HUMAN SOCIAL LEARNING

Humans emerged from their primate heritage by creating a new way to acquire knowledge and skills. That learning innovation involved extending the use of imitation beyond immediate kin to exceptional strangers-individuals who somehow excelled in the eyes of the family and the learner (often a developing child). While a juvenile monkey learns by imitating its mother and genetically related adults; human juveniles learn by imitating both genetically related adults (i.e., family members) *and* non-genetically-related individuals (i.e., anyone who captures the child's attention and trust). The extension of learning capacities beyond the immediate family circle allowed early human groups to identify exceptionally skilled individuals (e.g., hunters, healers, shamans, craftsmen etc.), and to benefit from the talents of these individuals.

Imitative learning is called 'social learning' in the scientific literature. It occurs via rote imitation, empathy, 'mind-reading' or the ability to guess what is going on in the mind of another, social-emotional attachment between teacher and pupil and through other processes as well (Byrne and Whiten, 1988; Miller and Dollard, 1941; Russon, 1997; Tomasello, Kruger, and Ratner, 1993; Whiten and Byrne, 1997; Zentall and Galef, 1988). All of these forms of learning require relatively high-level cognitive abilities, including the ability to imitate, simulate or model complex mental systems of other persons (Davies and Stone, 1995). For example, when a person wants to learn from or imitate a teacher, he or she must try to model the Mind (beliefs, desires, intentions etc) of the teacher in order to understand the teacher's point of view and intentions. Many scholars believe we use the so-called 'theory of Mind' cognitive system (ToMM) to simulate the intentions of others (see papers in Davies and Stone, 1995). If we call the Model "teacher" or "leader" then we can speak of teacher-student or leader-follower relations. Once the teacher's Mind is adequately 'modeled' by the student using the above psychologic processes, the imitator (student) can empathize with the teacher and thus see things from the teacher's perspective. This *perspective-taking ability* is the key component of the emulation process that allows one to imitate the mental states and thus the skills, behaviors and character of others (Meltzoff and Gopnik, 1993; Ruby and Decety, 2001; Zentall and Galef, 1988). Note that negative psychologic processes like envy would interfere with this key perspective-taking ability and thus would short-circuit any attempt to emulate a great leader.

How should we understand the process of emulation? Certainly the part of the ability to imitate appears to be in-born-witness the early imitation of the mother's facial expressions by the infant. But motor imitation of the acts of another are not quite what we mean by emulation. Emulation also involves the ability to feel what another is feeling. It involves sympathy and empathy and these high level abilities in turn involve the 'reading' of the Mind state of another. Clearly the mysterious capacity to empathize with another lies at the basis of emulation and empathy likely builds on the prior innate ability to imitate.

How does imitation work? Based on extensive research, Meltzoff and colleagues propose the Active Intermodal Mapping Hypothesis (AIM). The AIM is proposed to explain early facial imitation, and lay the groundwork for empathy and theory of Mind abilities (Meltzoff and Gopnik, 1993). According to the AIM, the object's expression is perceived and compared to the subject's own current expression (from proprioceptive feedback) in a supramodal representational space. The subject's efferent copy is compared to the object's afferent copy in this space, equivalences are detected and reduced, and imitation results. According to a perception-action view the perception of the object's expression *automatically* activates a similar motor expression in the subject (in contrast to AIM), but through a representation (in agreement with AIM). This expression could in turn be compared through feedback to the representation, and the difference between copies could be detected and reduced (in agreement with AIM).

Once you have the ability to imitate how do you develop empathy? Simulation theory has been proposed to be a mechanism for empathy, where the subject theorizes or guesses at the mental and emotional state of the object by simulating the object's state internally (Davies and Stone, 1995).

What supports these high-level imitation and empathy abilities? The discovery of so-called mirror neurons prompted a series of papers extending the possible function of these cells from the coding of simple motor acts, to the coding of other's mental states and these cells were suggested to provide evidence for simulation theory of empathy (reviewed in Rizzolatti, Fogassi, and Gallese, 2001). While mirror neurons alone cannot produce empathy at any level, they do provide concrete cellular evidence for the shared representations of perception and action that likely underlie empathy and similar imitation a-related abilities.

While mirror neurons likely do underlie some aspects of empathy, empathy itself often includes an emotional experience. Where does this emotional experience fit in? Natural, complex emotional situations require the activation of many complex factors, including episodic memories, autonomic sensation, and emotional valence. Because shared representations are networks of neurons that are interconnected, there is no one place in the brain where they exist.

In psychopathic or sociopathic individuals (the terms have been used interchangeably) we find an inability to experience normal states of empathy. There is a characteristic lack in sociopaths of normal autonomic responses to the distress cues of another, the social isolation, and the apparent disregard for the emotional and physical state of others. Moral reasoning is also impaired in sociopathic children, even controlling for cognitive development, IQ, or social class (Blair, 1995, 1997). Without the ability to be aroused by the distress of others, these individuals cannot understand and learn about the state of others through their own substrates.

Focal prefrontal cortex damage and closed-head injury in adults result in changes in empathy (reviewed by Eslinger, 1998). Patients with early-onset damage to the prefrontal cortex have a syndrome resembling psychopathy, with little or no empathy or remorse, a paucity of lasting social relationships, significant impairments on moral reasoning despite normal performance on intellectual tasks, and a deficient increase in skin conductance responses to risk in a gambling task (Anderson, Bechara, Damasio, Tranel, and Damasio, 1999). One of the two subjects studied by Anderson et al with early prefrontal damage was a mother marked by "dangerous insensitivity to the infant's needs" (Anderson et al., 1999, p. 1032). The authors propose a mechanism for the disorder whereby brain damage prevents patients from developing knowledge of the emotional sensitivity required for navigating and understanding social situations.

AREAS OF THE BRAIN THAT PARTICIPATE IN EMULATION AND IMITATIVE LEARNING

If, as the above considerations imply, that human social learning was influenced by standard selection and evolutionary forces, then the human brain should exhibit processing specializations consistent with requirements of imitative learning. There is now substantial evidence for this supposition (Barton and Dunbar, 1997; Gigerenzer, 1997; Gallese, Keysers, and Rizzolatti, 2004). As we have just seen, imitation and mimicry occurs via mediation of a series of neural networks involving so-called mirror neurons (Rizzolatti et al., 2001). Mirror neurons fire whenever the individual imitates the behaviors of a model. These neurons are found in areas of the inferior frontal cortex, the posterior parietal cortex, and in superior temporal cortex—all areas of the primate cortex most highly developed in humans. These are primary 'command areas' of the brain that influence all other behavioral processes such that they reliably recruit all of the other behavioral capacities of the individual and in short shape the character and behavior of the individual. The superior temporal cortex codes an early visual description of the action to be imitated and sends this information to posterior parietal *mirror* neurons. The posterior parietal cortex codes the precise kinesthetic aspect of the movement (i.e., translates the code into motor representation) and sends this information to inferior frontal mirror neurons. The inferior frontal cortex codes the goal of the action. Efferent copies of motor plans are, then sent from parietal and frontal mirror areas back to the superior temporal cortex, such that a matching mechanism between the visual description of the observed action and the predicted sensory consequences of the planned imitative action can occur. Once the visual description of the observed action and the predicted sensory consequences of the planned imitative action are matched, imitation can be initiated.

SPECIAL ROLE OF EMPATHY

Empathy involves the *inner imitation* of the actions and feelings and thoughts of others. Feeling the suffering or pain of another is particularly effective in generating empathy. In keeping with this concept, empathic individuals exhibit nonconscious mimicry of the postures, mannerisms, and facial expressions of others (the *chameleon effect*) to a greater extent than nonempathic individuals (Chartrand and Bargh, 1999).

Empathy and perspective taking crucially depend on the frontal lobes (Deckel, Hesselbrock, and Bauer, 1996; Eisenberg and Strayer, 1987; Ross, Homan, and Buck, 1994). Persons with orbitofrontal lesions are sometimes unable to experience empathy (Damasio, Tranel, and Damasio, 1991; Grattan, Bloomer, Archambault, and Eslinger, 1994). Sociopaths who perform poorly on tests of orbitofrontal function typically exhibit an inability to empathize with other's suffering (Damasio et al., 1991; Smith, Arnett, and Newman, 1992). They evidence serious deficits in expression of the social emotions (love, shame, guilt, empathy, and remorse). On the other hand, they are not intellectually handicapped, and are skillful manipulators of others (Davison and Neale, 1994).

In short, the cognitive neuroscience literature provides ample evidence for brain processing systems that specialize in support of the various functions implicated in emulation or imitative learning from 'theory of mind' attributions, to perspective taking and empathy. These systems include but are not limited to the anterior limbic and prefrontal networks responsible for behavioral autonomy (Lhermitte, 1986), executive function (Barkley, 1997), emotional regulation (Damasio, 1996) and interpersonal social interactions.

The brain data speak to the ancient evolutionary roots and power of imitative learning as well as the central role of social interactions in the creation of human nature. We all possess powerful social learning capacities that operate virtually automatically and involuntarily. Interpersonal empathy is central to social learning and to human nature. It is the linchpin between learning and leading that makes emulation and leadership possible. The ancient philosophers understood that these powerful learning capacities could be harnessed for good or ill –depending on the teachers available to aspiring students or followers.

In his "Parallel Lives", Plutarch repeatedly called attention to a kind of noble grandeur and audacity of spirit that we only rarely find in today's' leaders. We need to find such individuals in history if we cannot find them among the living. If we do not find worthy models, the compulsive nature of imitative learning processes will ensure that we will involuntarily imitate unworthy models. Everything depends therefore on whom we choose to imitate. If we surround ourselves with persons who refuse leadership responsibilities we will tend to imitate that kind of response. If we refuse to learn the histories of the great men and women of the past our personalities will to that extent be impoverished. Plutarch understood this and gave us the finest compendium of parallel lives ever assembled. He invites us to consider emulation of the best of these characters and to learn from the rest.

But before we return to our illustrious examples, we ought to complete mapping of the human mind and consider the role of intelligence in the rise of leaders among early humans. Intelligence will be examined from its most basic aspect as problem solving, to its more complex role in support of political, strategic and social interactions—all crucial forms of intelligence for the leader.

Chapter 4

LEADERSHIP AND SOCIAL INTELLIGENCE

INTRODUCTION

We have seen how both prestige and political dominance including the ability to punish free-riders was essential to early leaders. We have also seen that there may have been evolutionary pressures for leaders to develop strong character traits of trustworthiness, morality, reliability etc as these hard-to-fake character strengths marked out the individual as someone with whom you could do business with and flourish! We now wish to add to the list of traits that pick out effective leaders. These traits it must be emphasized were absolutely essential to the identification of trustworthy leaders and thus to the emergence of effective forms of cooperation in early human societies.

Among the more reliable markers of leadership capability must be the trait we call 'intelligence'. From our evolutionary and communications perspective, intelligence is clearly a hard-to-fake signal or character trait and we can therefore predict that leaders will attempt to develop this trait in order to distinguish themselves from competitors and to outwit their opponents. Intelligence in a potential leader would also allow potential followers to more easily identify potential trustworthy leaders. It would also allow leaders to successfully lead. It is clear that leadership of a group of unruly, suspicious individuals who face some challenge (e.g., a hunt, a war or a trek in the case of early humans) will require wisdom and intelligence if the cooperative enterprise is to succeed. A would-be leader cannot afford to fail or to develop a reputation of failure if he is to stay 'on top' in his role as leader. To succeed the leader has to become a teacher of his followers. He has to show his followers how to cooperate on the hunt or how to stay alive over long migratory treks or how to defend themselves against attacks or how to fashion weapons and tools and so forth. Thus the ability to teach and a native intelligence are crucial for a leader.

Do we in fact find higher average levels of intelligence among leaders? First it should be noted that intelligence itself is a complex trait that is difficult to measure objectively. Nevertheless, a consensus among scientists who study intelligence and talent seems to be emerging which suggests that a significant proportion of the variance in performance on intelligence scales is explicable in terms of genetically-related innate capacities. There are of course many forms of intelligence and many of these intelligence tests measure verbal forms of intelligence more accurately than other more emotionally-linked forms of intelligence. Nevertheless, most workers in the field would agree that some general creative problem solving abilities can be accurately described as a form of general intelligence and that this general intelligence is genetically influenced. General intelligence is thought to give you basic tools to excel at some domain that piques your interest.

General intelligence, (sometimes called Spearman's *g*) exhibits one of the largest heritability coefficients of all psychological traits, and the quantitative trait loci associated with gifted-level intelligence quotients or IQs are now being successfully located in the human chromosome (Chorney et al., 1998). At the same time, general intelligence is indubitably the individual-difference factor most consistently associated with (a) the ability to acquire expertise on complex tasks and (b) the capacity to display high-level performance in such domains as creativity and leadership (Simonton, 1995). In general, it would probably be the exception rather than the rule to find an established correlate of attainment in some talent domain that does not feature a nontrivial genetic substrate.

General intelligence is a prerequisite for talent and creativity in any performance domain. Simonton (1999) defined talent as any innate capacity that enables an individual to display exceptionally high performance in a domain that requires special skills and training. The capacity is considered to be innate when it consists of one or more components that feature substantial or nontrivial heritability coefficients. A heritability coefficient is a number between 0 and 1 which is typically derived from twin studies. Heritability estimates tend to run in the .40 - .60 range. These are considered moderate heritability coefficients. A moderate heritability for a trait does not mean that there is a gene for that trait. The influence is quantitative, that is there are many genes acting within the context of an environment that supports the development of the trait. An appropriate social context is needed to elicit innate talents or intelligences.

In sum, some measurable components of intelligence appear to be biologically influenced and heritable. This conclusion is consistent with the claims we make below: that a co-evolutionary process occurred between the evolution of greater and greater levels of intelligence among early humans on the one hand and the rise of exceptional individuals who took on specialized or leadership roles with respect to some cooperative enterprise on the other. The process, however, was undoubtedly complex.

COMPLEXITY OF LEADERSHIP

In early human groups it is likely that no single trait identified a good leader. Even today leadership is multiply influenced by several sets of factors and competencies including cognitive skills, personality dispositions, motivational orientations, long term behavioral habits, philosophical and religious values and, finally, situationally or contextually determined factors that interact with these aforementioned trait-related factors to yield leadership emergence and effectiveness. We assume along with Chen et al. (2000) and Zacarro et al. (2004) that individual differences in behavioral styles and competencies, including talent for leadership, can be divided up into traits that are more distal (distant) to behavioral performance and those that are more proximal (closer) to performance. Distal traits are less bound to current context than are proximal traits. Distal traits are more stable across time and context than are proximal traits. General cognitive abilities, motivation and personality are considered to be distal traits that a leader brings to each situation he or she faces while problem-solving and social-interaction skills are more proximal traits that the situation imposes on the leader. Each 'situation' will present a different problem and a different set of people whose needs must be taken into account, to the leader.

Mumford et al. (2000) and Zacarro et al. (2004) presented a model of leader characteristics and performance that takes into account the complexity of internal and external forces that determine leadership emergence and effectiveness. In their model, measures of cognitive, personality and motivation were significant distal predictors of leader social appraisal skills, problem solving skills, and expertise which in turn predicted leader performance. In the model, situational influences (the leader's operating environment) determine the quality and appropriateness of the leader's performance. In short, leadership emergence and effectiveness reflects the combined influence of distal and proximal personal traits interacting with the leader's operating environment which constrains choices and responses. Presumably, innate talent can be subsumed under the 'distal' trait category in this model.

In support of the Mumford and Zacarro multivariate model of leadership emergence/effectiveness is the wealth of studies (reviewed in Zacarro et al., 2004) linking general intelligence/cognitive ability with leadership emergence scores, management effectiveness, and overall leader performance. Successful leaders score consistently higher on intelligence scales and on cognitive complexity scales than do non-leaders or poor leaders. We can safely conclude then that however complex leadership is, leaders themselves are on average very intelligent individuals.

What then are the evolutionary roots of this relationship between leadership and intelligence? To answer this question we first need to discuss more thoroughly than we have in previous chapters the concept of social learning.

SOCIAL LEARNING

Social learning is 'imitative' or 'cultural learning'. It occurs in several social-cultural contexts such as social imitation, empathy, 'mind-reading' or reading the intentions of another (sometimes called 'theory of Mind' abilities), social-emotional attachment between teacher and pupil and so on. All of these forms of social learning require relatively high-level cognitive abilities, including the ability to simulate or model complex mental systems of other persons (Davies and Stone, 1995).

EVOLUTION OF SOCIAL LEARNING

Several scholars (Barton and Dunbar, 1997; Byrne and Whiten, 1988; Humphrey, 1976; Whiten and Byrne, 1997) have argued that an important driving force in the evolution of human intelligence has been the intense *social* forces that characterized, and still characterizes, both human and non-human primate societies. The struggle for early social attachment during the juvenile period, the later dependence on local social coalitions, the ever-shifting social alliances, the need to guard against social manipulation, the limitless forms of social cooperation and so forth, all placed a premium on the ability to 'deal' with others and to predict the social and mental abilities of others who could become partners or competitors. Competitive and cooperative forms of social relations require new and powerful forms of socially-based learning abilities (Zentall and Galef, 1988) and thus potentially could have fueled the evolution of advanced intelligence in humans. While there is no space to review it here, the available evidence, in fact, largely supports this hypothesis (Barton and Dunbar, 1997; Boyd and Richerson, 1988; Hauser, 1988; Premack and Premack, 1995; Russon, 1997; Tomasello, Kruger, and Ratner, 1993; Whiten and Byrne, 1997) and its corollary-that the expansion and functional make-up of the brain itself was driven in large measure by these same social demands (Banyas, 1999; Barton and Dunbar, 1997; Brothers, 1999).

It is not known, however, exactly how such intense social demands actually increased intelligence. Given the relatively short time (roughly 200,000 years) anatomically modern humans have been active, increased social intelligence had to be achieved through social forms of learning such as, teaching, imitation and the exploitation of the expertise of others, where rates of transfer of skills across individuals and generations were much faster than standard evolutionary rates (Pfeiffer, 1982; Tomasello et al., 1993; Zentall and Galef, 1988). There is fairly good evidence from observations of primate societies, cognitive development in human children and mathematical modeling of effects of social learning on cultural innovation that support the claim that imitative learning was key for the evolution of human intelligence (Boyd and Richerson, 1988; Hauser, 1988; Meltzoff and Gopnik, 1993; Parker and Gibson, 1991; Tomasello et al., 1993; Whiten and Byrne, 1997).

ROOTS OF SOCIAL LEARNING

How, then, did this kind of imitative learning evolve in our ancestral societies? For most primates, apparently, imitative learning takes place primarily within the parent-child context (Hauser, 1988; Russon, 1997). *For humans, however, such learning regularly takes place both within and outside of the parent-child context* (Hauser, 1988; Russon, 1997; Tomasello et al., 1993; Zentall and Galef, 1988). We can assume that in 'allowing' imitative learning to take place outside of the parent-child context: 1) early humans opened up the possibility that some individuals could specialize in the act of learning itself (become 'culture-bearers') even after maturity had been reached, 2) new skills, not typically acquired in the parent child context, i.e. skills some steps removed from immediate developmental imperatives, could now be more easily acquired, and 3) an emphasis was placed on identifying talent in potential teachers. Here is where the leader as teacher enters the picture. If teachers could be found, apprenticeships could be developed and whole new areas of expertise, in hunting, clothing manufactures, tool-making, crafts, weapons, knowledge about plants, the healing arts etc could flourish.

All depended, of course, on finding a social form outside of the parent-child complex that promoted opportunities for imitative learning. Such a form of learning that took place outside of the parent-child context would likely carry-over both positive and negative aspects of the parent-child relationship such as extreme dependency, excessive devotion, extreme open-ness to being guided etc. as these characteristics that would facilitate learning. Obviously many of these negative forms of dependency still occur in followers, particularly of unscrupulous leaders.

The emphasis on cultural learning would also promote an intense urge to find exceptional teachers/leaders as benefits of social learning depended on the quality of the teachers involved.

EARLY TEACHER/LEADERS AND THE ORIGINS OF CHARISMATIC LEADERSHIP

Proto-forms of leadership very likely involved teaching as social learning may have provided the forum for individuals to specialize in imitative learning; i.e., to spend large amounts of time as a 'student' outside of the parent-child context. The better the quality of the teacher the more 'students' he would attract. Thus charismatic teachers would become particularly successful. There is abundant anthropological and archeological evidence (e.g., Mumford, 1966; Rappaport, 1999; Weber, 1946; but see Durkheim, 1912/1995) that points to the generative potential of charismatic teachers (and by implication 'students') for the roots of cooperation, particularly in the forms of religious ritual. Certainly, the religious behaviors of pre-modern tribal peoples often involved identification of individuals who were thought to possess charisma, manna, power etc and then the elevation of such individuals to shaman status or to leadership roles in the tribal councils.

The root form of the leader-follower relationship, at least in so far as it involved a teaching function was therefore probably a kind of 'Master-disciples' relationship, where a group of postulants gathered round a charismatic individual who exhibited a range of exceptional abilities. The 'disciples' would observe, imitate and exploit the expertise of the 'Master'. The 'Master', in turn, would benefit from the help and praise of his or her disciples. While the initial learning focus was probably utilitarian it is likely that the need to exalt the powers or knowledge of the teacher soon led to an emphasis on non-utilitarian matters as well.

THE MASTER-DISCIPLE RELATION AS AN EVOLUTIONARILY-STABLE STRATEGY

Given the fact that the Master/teacher had to be a person of exceptional intelligence or social abilities, the leader-follower relation would theoretically increase the reproductive rates of *both parties*-the disciples and the Master. The Master gets all the added help from the disciples, while the disciples get the association with an exceptionally talented person, and therefore a more efficient resource acquisition strategy than their own. The end result of this specialized form of cooperation would be more resources for each individual in the Master-disciples group. The individuals in the 'leader's coalition', furthermore, would have an advantage over individuals in other social-coalitions because its roles (master versus disciples) were more clearly defined (via ritual) and the ties between individuals in the alliance itself were more firmly cemented by the nature of the relation (i.e., its intense emotionality and the devotion to the Master).

RITUAL, COSTLY SIGNALS AND THE IDENTIFICATION OF INDIVIDUALS WITH EXCEPTIONAL CHARACTERISTICS

Theoretically, the ability to learn from individuals with anomalous or superior cognitive abilities will lead to increased chances at obtaining better resources and thus increased reproductive success. Natural selection will therefore favor development of special propensities to look-for, detect, predict and become receptive to extraordinary mental qualities in others. There is, in fact, experimental evidence that suggests that children, particularly adolescents, are endowed with an innate tendency to look for and be receptive to talented or charismatic or unusual agents including 'supernatural' agents (Barrett, Richert, and Driesenga, 2001).

What are the signals we use to identify supra-normal abilities and individuals? How did our ancestors choose the best teachers? While simple observation of 'who's currently got the resources' will count in such an assessment, better assessments, particularly for long-lived social primates with prolonged juvenile dependency periods like ourselves, will require identification of who will *consistently be successful* in acquiring resources over long periods of time.

One way to identify a potential 'teacher' would be to choose someone already identified as such by others. So once again reputation becomes important. But again reputation is not enough. Reputation needs to be backed up by costly signals. If you saw someone treated with extreme deference and ritual displays of praise and homage you would conclude that the person was probably an exceptionally gifted person. Thus, *ritual itself* would advertise the identification of exceptional individuals. It is in the interest of both the disciples and the Master to advertise the charismatic power of the Master so as to discourage competitors and opponents, as well as to attract new partners (disciples) and potential mates. Thus, the extreme importance of ritual for the evolution of leadership and of social learning.

The above considerations underline both the immense trust placed in leaders by early humans and the immense dangers that that trust and dependency creates when the leader turns out to have a less than sterling character. In our view the mark of a good leader is that the leader understands the sacred trust that has been placed in him by his followers. The wise leader will therefore become a great teacher. He will attempt to undercut the negative effects of the ancient tendency to become dependent on leaders and instead cultivate leadership qualities in his followers. The crux, therefore of the leader-follower relationship lies in the ability of the leader to model integrity, intelligence, wisdom and honesty for his followers. The wise prestige-oriented leader in short will draw on the social learning instincts of his followers to elicit emulation of his best character traits in order to turn followers into leaders.

In our discussion to this point we have posited a theory on how early human groups may have identified leaders as those individuals who were of good character and sterling reputation. In chapters to follow we will start looking at some higher-level traits that will bring us very close to the classical virtues, and so, back to our examples of Plutarchan heroes from history.

Chapter 5

LANGUAGE, RHETORIC AND LEADERSHIP

INTRODUCTION

Our evolutionary approach to the leader-follower relationship has emphasized the importance of leader-related traits of intelligence, trustworthiness, reliability and political skill. How do followers choose leaders? They do so by identifying individuals who display the aforementioned traits. Thus it is all important for the leader to develop these abilities and traits –else he or she will never be selected to lead. Followers, to some extent create leaders. Leaders make themselves to the extent to which they develop the traits that followers identify as necessary in a leader.

We have also emphasized two basic leadership strategies leaders have evolved in response to follower demands. The first strategy is political dominance. While it is ultimately backed up by some form of authority, force and power, the dominance strategy is best exemplified by the master manipulator and politician who can dominate a group of followers or a set of opponents simply by outwitting or outmaneuvering them politically. A good leader can, for example, neutralize the negative effects of the free-rider by punishing the free-riders and preventing their access to the cooperative enterprises of the group. The cooperative members of the group can then trust that their efforts will not be exploited and thus the whole enterprise will benefit.

The second major strategy leaders employ to elicit followers and to neutralize opponents is the prestige-oriented strategy. A prestigious individual can easily attract followers and lead them effectively if he uses his intelligence, his good reputation and his organizational and political abilities. An essential key tool for the leader, especially the prestige-oriented leader is language. He must be a master at use of language in order to effectively lead people; keep followers engaged and on-task; and turn followers into leaders themselves. In Chapter One we listed seven trait-related characteristics of men of eminence in the ancient world as identified by Plutarch. One of the most important of these characteristics was the cultivation of rhetoric or the ability to speak well in public.

With an effective use of language the leader en-nobles his followers by communicating the leader's conception of a just and productive order. The leader moves his followers to strive for that vision of a finely ordered society. The primary tool used by a leader to communicate his vision of a just and finely ordered society or team or organization etc is language. When language is used in this way, i.e., in a way that elevates and inspires followers, we call it rhetoric.

We will therefore need to investigate the ways in which leaders use rhetoric to recruit, educate, persuade, nourish and direct followers. A leader's skill with language as a tool to direct followers and forestall opponents is a primary measure of the leader's ability to lead.

And so we ask how do leaders use language in order to effect change? How do leaders use language to prevent passivity in followers? How do leaders use language in order to promote cooperative enterprises? How do leaders use language to quell opposition? We will attempt to answer these questions by bringing the tools of evolutionary psychology to bear on the issues and by examining Plutarch's treatment of these topics in the lives he examines in his biographic analyses. Before we turn to those magnificent Plutarchan analyses of the power of rhetoric, we wish to first sketch the evolutionary background of the dependence of leaders on effective use of language to attain to leadership roles.

The best leaders use language well. This link between effective language use and effective leadership gives us a clue to the evolutionary origins of leadership itself. We argue that persons who could use language well acquired prestige, status and followers and thus de facto leadership. Our contention in this chapter will be that effective language use was one of the characteristics in early human groups to mark a person off as 'special'. In short, mastery of effective use of language in small groups of early humans was one of the crucial factors in the rise of the leader-follower social relationship in human evolution. We further argue that the evolution of language itself was tied to its usefulness in conferring social prestige on an individual…that language evolved, in part, because it was able to confer reproductive benefits on those who could best make use of it. The evolution of language led to the evolution of leadership and the evolution of leadership provided further impetus for the evolution of key properties of language and so forth.

We realize that these claims concerning the impact of language use on language evolution may be controversial. This claim however says nothing about the origins of proto-language…of how language evolved in the first place. We merely claim that once some sort of proto-language was available to early humans it became one of the forces that drove the evolution of leaders. The way in which it did this was simple: effective use of proto-language conferred prestige on the person displaying these unusual powers and prestige always translated into greater reproductive benefits in early human societies. In order to situate our claims within the broader evolutionary history of language we first summarize some of thinking on the early origins of language. We will see that the picture is complex.

LANGUAGE EVOLUTION

Human language of course is complex, arising from at least three distinct but interacting adaptive systems: 1) individual social learning (via interactions with the mother during the juvenile period and then with others), 2) cultural transmission via interactions with the rest of the group, and 3) biological evolution (via genetic and brain systems). Models of language evolution which incorporate these three sources of change best accommodate the facts concerning language use and language properties as we know them today. But how did the first proto-language evolve to begin with? There had to be 'pre-adaptations'-or innate capacities that helped early populations acquire a proto-language. A major constraint on the evolution of language properties-once the proto-language appeared, is that the properties must be 'learnable' by the child. After all language is acquired by most humans by the time they are 2-4 years old. To accomplish that feat the child must come pre-adapted or 'ready-made' to acquire language. If there is some feature of language that must be acquired by every child, then a child who is born already knowing (preadapted) that feature will be at an advantage. This is the fundamental mechanism of genetic assimilation or the 'Baldwin Effect' whereby learned behaviors can become innate.

So what were some of the preadaptations that early hominids possessed or learned so that the first proto-language could evolve and then later be acquired by every human child? One preadaptation that occurred in the hominid lineage (among the apes) was the ability to use symbols. Symbol use is typically construed as a capacity for linking sounds or gestures arbitrarily to specific concepts and/or percepts – in particular for the purpose of communication. In addition, it has been suggested that the ability to relate these symbols to each other sequentially…to link them up in a series …and then have the series refer to some object in the world…i.e. to convey meaning…was a further necessary preadaptation for language. Although there is evidence that nonhuman primates have some capacity, albeit limited, for using sequences of arbitrary symbols in captivity there is considerable debate over whether they use these symbols to refer to things in nature. Therefore, the use of complex sequences of symbols to refer to objects and situations may be a uniquely human ability. Other preadaptations for acquisition of language in the child are "Joint attention" – that is, the capacity of the infant or child to follow the eye-gaze direction of the mother who can then direct the attention of the child to a specific significant object. The child must intuit that whatever the mother is looking at she must be thinking about and thus the child begins to learn how to read the mind and intentions of the mother. We discussed this 'theory of Mind' ability in a previous chapter.

Another potential social pre-adaptation for language is the capability of modern humans for sophisticated imitation of action sequences for the purpose of communication. Our ability to represent others as intentional beings with their own beliefs and desires, which can be manipulated by our actions, may also be a social prerequisite for language. Again we discussed social imitation and emulation abilities in a previous chapter. Absent the ability to internally imitate or model the intentions and beliefs of others no sharing of information via language would be possible. We will see below that the sharing of information relevant to the concerns of the speakers was a crucially important force in the evolution of language use.

What about the formal properties of language itself? Language fundamentally links spoken sounds (phonemes) to meaning via grammatical rules (we set aside written language for now on the grounds that it probably did not evolve until quite late in hominid evolution; i.e. in the last 5000 years). We have already referred to the role of symbols in language. This is the property of 'displacement' -a word can point to something in the world that is currently not present. Within a sentence displacement refers to the fact that phrases may be dislocated from their natural argument or thematic roles. Every sentence for example can be decomposed into so-called thematic roles such as, who did what to whom, when, where, and why. These abstract mental 'slots' or thematic roles may have been a preadaptation. The order in which they occur across languages is rule-governed though the rules vary somewhat from language to language. Language also exhibits 'structure dependence'…the subject must come before the object in certain types of language and the order of these thematic roles matters for language use and interpretation. The grammar of language –its structure dependence or syntax- is influenced by both biologic and cultural transmission. Specific grammatical disorders can sometimes be linked to specific genetic mutations (indicating the biologic influence) and evidence that growth of language complexity linked to growth of cultural complexity indicates the influence of cultural transmission. Another syntax-related property of language is its compositionality or its recursive generative capacity. Since it is composed of these fundamental thematic roles (Noun, subject, object, verb, argument etc) these primary constituents can be combined (by strictly defined rules) in an infinite number of ways to convey an infinite number of meanings. Consider that with the finite vocabulary and a finite number of rules you can, via various re-combinations of the basic words and thematic slots, generate an infinite number of sentences that convey an equally infinite number of meanings. In short, language is a device for the production of an infinite number of meanings in a medium that allows for the communication of these infinite meanings to another who uses similar words and rules. We will see below that this information-sharing capacity of language has important consequences for the rise of the leadership phenomena among early humans as well as the leader – follower social relation.

ROLE OF SOCIAL IMITATION IN
EVOLUTION OF THE PROTO-LANGUAGE

We have emphasized in a previous chapter the role of emulation in the leader-follower relationship. Here we argue that emulation played a role as well in the evolution of the proto-language. Because vocal communication in primates is largely affective in nature and with little voluntary control, some investigators have claimed that language use in humans is likely to have emerged from manual gestures rather than primate calls. In some versions of this account, the emergence of gestural language was predated by the evolution of a unique human ability for complex imitation. Gestural imitation in the infant/child (such as pointing to an object of shared attention) predates the emergence of language abilities. Once again we see the crucial role of imitation in human social learning. The subsequent change from a gestural to a primarily vocal language in the species has been argued to be due to either increased tool use coming into conflict with the use of the hands for linguistic gestures or the 'recruitment' of vocalization through associations between gesture and sound. In any case whether through gesture or sound or both people could understand one another's intentions by internally trying to imitate the gestures or sounds of the other. The imitation would to some extent re-produce the emotions or the intentions of the model and thus two individuals could learn that they share (or do not share) the same intentions etc. Individuals who could not imitate the calls or gestures of their conspecifics would be at a disadvantage when parties started to congregate for cooperative enterprises such as hunting etc. The need for advanced imitation abilities in early humans also had an impact on brain capacities/structures. We spoke in an earlier chapter of the recently discovered mirror-neuron system which mediates complex imitative actions in apes and humans. These mirror-neuron systems appear to be dedicated to supporting the functions of imitation and emulation

Once the proto-language emerged it began to be exploited by individuals to increase their own reproductive fitness. They started to use language to form alliances with others, to predict the behaviors and intentions of others, to share information with others in an altruistic way and so forth. Effective use of language then began to have an impact on how language itself evolved as well. In effect we can detect the impact of leaders in early human groups by observing their effects on language properties. The individuals who used language to best effect (to increase their own fitness and to assist others in doing so) were the 'leaders'. We argue that one of the first distinguishing marks of a leader was his or her ability to use language effectively...to advance the cooperative interests of the group via use of language. When language is used to persuade others to engage in some cooperative enterprise we call it rhetoric.

The primary impact of leaders on language properties falls in the realm of what is today called 'pragmatics'. Pragmatics is the study of how language is used across varying social contexts. Sperber and Wilson (2002) have argued that the primary property that defines effective and appropriate use of language in any given social context is 'relevance'. Listeners are thought of as constantly asking themselves 'To what extent is the speaker's language or conversation relevant to the issue at hand?' The greater the relevance of the information content in the speaker's language, the more appropriate it is to the context and the more effective it will be for the listener. Listener's track 'relevance' and speakers attempt to be 'relevant'. The greater the relevance, the greater the impact the speaker has on the listeners and on social context. The greater the relevance the greater the speaker's social prestige.

So how do we define relevance then? Sperber and Wilson suggest that relevance is a measure of information content ...the greater the relevance the more inferences the listener can engage in...in short, the more the listener learns from the speaker the more the speaker's discourse is considered relevant. The greater the relevance, the greater the speaker's prestige.

When a speaker conveys information I can measure the information content of that speech by testing whether it allows me to derive, via inferential reasoning, new information, new knowledge. If the speaker gives me new knowledge then that is a resource I can use and the speaker's status is thereby increased. But relevance requires fine tuning by the speaker: too little information and he loses his audience (because they cannot derive enough new knowledge). Too much information and inferential chains become too extended, reasoning breaks down and once again too little new knowledge is produced. So how does the speaker produce a speech containing just the right amount of relevance? The short answer is 'via the rules of rhetoric'.

In the classical world (and right up until the high middle ages) rhetoric was considered one of the three original liberal arts or *trivium* (the other members being dialectic and grammar). Grammar involved the study of the production of syntactically correct and effective sentences. What was correct was determined through the study and criticism of literary models. Dialectic was a process of argument involving presentation of a claim or thesis, then consideration of its anti-thesis and finally production of a synthesis of the two claims. Rhetoric, on the other hand, was concerned solely with the study of manipulation of others via effective and persuasive speech in public and political settings such as assemblies and courts of law.

Under the study of rhetoric a student would learn that every persuasive speech involves a period of preparation and research (invention or *inventio*) that was crucial for development and refinement of the argument to be made in the speech. Once arguments were developed, the student learned to arrange them in most logical and effective order (*dispositio*). That order would typically begin with an *exordium* or prologue that would underline the significance of the speech the audience would soon hear. Then would come the major and minor arguments presented in logical order without any unnecessary detail. Objections would be anticipated and dealt with in each step of the major arguments. Once placement of the major and minor arguments were decided upon the student would then read through the speech and attend to matters of *elocutio* (style) and *pronuntiatio* (presentation). After these matters of content and style were decided the speech had to be memorized (*Memoria*) using the highly developed 'arts of memory' or memorization available to the ancient scholar and leader. Finally the speech had to be practiced and then delivered to an audience (Actio).

LANGUAGE USE AND RHETORIC

The ability to speak well in public was a supreme leadership virtue for Plutarch. Among the great speakers of the ancient world, the best remembered today are Cicero the Roman and Demosthenes the Athenian.

Of Cicero, Plutarch writes (Life of Cicero, 13) how his eloquence contributed to the invincibility of justice. Plutarch notes both Cicero's natural gift for well-reasoned speech as well as the pains he took to develop eloquence through study of diction and rhetoric (Life of Cicero, 3) Likewise in the Life of Demosthenes (Life of Demosthenes, 7-8) Plutarch details the course of study and discipline of practice by means of which Demosthenes rose to become the best orator of his age.

Plutarch shows how these great orators learned to speak well and it turns out to be a remarkably simple process of practicing in public, first in small venues and building up to larger audiences regardless of fear. The effective speaker did not appeal to the lowest instincts of the crowd but instead, grabbed the crowd's attention and elevated it, such that each individual in the crowd could see the role he was called upon to play to further the noble aims of the group. However, it is not enough to speak well; one must speak with a force that is persuasive in getting the hearers to act.

Plutarch, ever looking for the practical skills of leadership in his subjects, acknowledges that Demosthenes was, indeed, the best orator of his time, but Phocion the most powerful speaker. While Demosthenes' Philippics, or speeches against Philip of Macedon are still looked to as examples of rhetorical flair, he was quite ineffective in his goal of preserving Athenian independence from Macedonian rule. Rather, by stirring up the Athenians against Philip, he set them on a ruinous course of war that would lead to defeat at the hands of Philip's son, Alexander the Great. And Demosthenes' conduct belied his bellicose talk, for in the heat of battle, the very battle he had brought on by his inflammatory speeches, he fled, a coward. In contrast, Phocion, tried to reason with the Athenians to accept a working accommodation with Alexander and his successors rather than renew an unwinnable war. Finding the people intractable, Phocion accepts the inevitable and makes the most powerful statement of all by accepting death rather than compromise with untruth, proclaiming (Life of Phocion, 9) "You may compel me to act against my wishes, but you shall never force me to speak against my judgment."

Plutarch further argues for the power of the word when he has Pyrrhus, the Greek commander whose name has become a byword for victory gained at unacceptably high cost, say, that his friend Cineas, the disciple of Demosthenes had taken more towns with his words, than Pyrrhus did with his arms.

Howard Gardner (1995) in his "Leading Minds' talked about effective language use as one of the defining attributes of the good leader. Gardner claimed that leaders achieve their effectiveness chiefly through the stories they relate. Chief among these stories are 'stories of identity' – narratives that help individuals think about and feel who they are, where they come from, and where they are headed. Effective use of rhetoric in other words helps to orient a people; it gives the people a direction, a meaning and yes, an identity.

In addition to the examples above we will examine the role of rhetoric in the rise to leadership in the life of Cicero in a future chapter. But first we need to complete the evolutionary sketch of the link between language use and prestige in early modern humans in order to understand why it was that Cicero had the success he did in his career.

Why do we defer to someone who uses language well versus someone who does not? The answer is rooted in the past. Masterly use of language indicated to our evolutionary forebears that the speaker possessed intelligence, wisdom, important information that concerned the welfare of the listener ("relevance") and altruistic intent (since the speaker was sharing this information with the listener). Masterly use of language therefore conferred prestige on the speaker and this prestige contributed to the speaker's leadership credentials. We now review the logic and evidence of this claim.

RELEVANCE

Linguists have asserted that many of the formal properties of language use flow from the principle of 'relevance' (Sperber and Wilson, 1995, 2002; Strawson, 1964). This basic principle of human communication states that in order for a speaker's contribution to a conversation to be well-formed or felicitous, it should pertain to or add information to the matter at hand or to the topic currently under discussion. Speaker's contributions should have high information content where the value of the information is measured in terms of the topic at hand. Dessalles (1998) summarizes the relevance principle this way: "An utterance must either refer to a problematic situation or attempt to reduce the problematicity of a situation" (p.133). Irrelevant contributions will be considered beside the point or even annoying and therefore they will be ignored and even may be considered grounds for excluding the speaker from the conversation altogether.

To be a player in a conversation, therefore, your contributions to the conversation must be relevant. Although this observation may strike the reader as blindingly obvious a number of important consequences for the evolution of both language and human social interactions flow from it. First, please note that people vary in their ability to contribute relevant information to a conversation. This variance is due to many factors. Some people may be more intelligent or more fluent etc. Or someone may just by chance possess information that is highly relevant to some problem the local group or tribe is currently facing. Or someone might possess relevant information to most of the tribe's current needs/desires because that person has access to information from many sources in the group. He is considered a friend to many people in the group and therefore people share with him their goals/desires and their 'important information'. This person who has friends throughout the tribe will therefore possess a great store of valuable and relevant information for people in the tribe and his contributions to most conversations in the group will possess a priori relevance for any conversation taken at random from the pool of daily conversations occurring in the tribe.

The information-drive component of the relevance criterion presumably created some amount of competition among speakers allowing "relevance' to become linked to speaker quality. The person who could acquire the greatest quantity of relevant information would thereby increase his prestige, the number of his followers and the number of cooperative alliances he could enter into. Because relevance became linked to 'resource holding potential' the competition to attain to relevance likely became and remained intense in early human communities. Relevant information had to be updated and enhanced constantly precisely in order to remain relevant and to stay ahead of the competition. Individuals would therefore require impressive memory abilities and these in turn would eventually lead to greater levels of intelligence.

Although the relevance constraint likely led to greater overall and generalized forms of intelligence in early humans (particularly among leaders) the relevance criterion also likely led to specialized forms of expertise as well. The relevance criterion is inherently context-sensitive. For information to be relevant it has to help solve a specific problem in a specific place and time. Take for example, the problem of illness. There is a child who is feverish, dehydrated and dying. You could be highly intelligent with large stores of tribal lore and wisdom and even be considered a leader of the tribe, but if you could not contribute to the amelioration of the illness of the child your contributions to discussions about the child would not be considered relevant. The lowliest tribesman with an herbal remedy or a Shaman with his incantations would possess greater prestige in this situation than would the leader of the tribe. The link between technical intelligence, relevance and prestige would therefore make its contribution to the rise of such worthy attainments as democracy and intelligence among early humans.

Our concern here however is the role of the 'relevance constraint' in the rise of the leader-follower social relation. The link is simple: Once relevance could be used by listeners to identify persons of quality, relevance likely became a criterion people would use when deciding who they would affiliate with, cooperate with and follow. Then as relevance grew in importance so did rhetoric or the ability to display relevance in an eloquent speech, story or communication. Thus, pursuit of information (and with it relevance) created competition among would-be leaders. The competition was to become the most 'relevant' person in the tribe. Those individuals who could demonstrate the greatest intelligence, the greatest eloquence, the greatest story-telling ability or the greatest technical know-how would possess the most relevant information content and therefore great prestige. He who could best convey valuable information most efficiently and/or eloquently to listeners etc would attain high status and prestige. To stay on top (to stay relevant) however the leader would have to continuously update his informational sources and content. Only those individuals with the most prodigious memories and the greatest intelligence could succeed and succeed consistently.

RELEVANCE AND ALTRUISM

We noted in a previous chapter that one function of the leader was promotion of order and cooperation among group members. We also noted that group cooperation always had to solve the problem of the social parasite or free-rider in order to the cooperative enterprise to succeed. Group members would decline to participate in any cooperative enterprise if they felt that their labors and exertions were going to be exploited by an unscrupulous individual or individuals who gained the benefits of the cooperative enterprise without incurring any of the costs. The leader helps to solve this problem of the free-rider by taking on the role of the 'enforcer' of group norms and by agreeing to punish the free-rider—often at a cost to his own fitness etc. Another way that the leader contributes to the order and cooperation among tribal members is via relevance.

Please note that the provision of valuable information to a group of interested individuals is an altruistic act --performed by the person contributing the information. The individual who approaches a group of worried individuals who are discussing the smoke seen beyond the hills and informs them that that smoke is due to raiding parties headed in their direction would have reason to thank the individual who provided that highly relevant information. Therefore anybody who can consistently provide valuable/relevant information to a conversation will be marked as an altruistic person—someone you would want to cooperate with (and not a free-rider). This is another source of the prestige attached to persons who exhibit high relevance in conversations.

RELEVANCE IMPOSES STRUCTURE ON CONVERSATIONS

In order to convey highly relevant information most effectively a speaker must tailor his message to the interests and abilities of the listeners. The speaker must find ways to reveal his intentions and meanings to the speakers. He must try to minimize the interpretative work the listener needs to perform in order to quickly and efficiently grasp the information content of his speech. Sperber and Wilson even made this aspect of the relevance constraint one of the criterion measures of a message's 'relevance'. Those messages/utterances are relevant to the extent that the message activates or produces a chain of inferences in the Minds of the listeners. The speaker wants the listener to think about his message… but not too much. Too little inferencing on the part of the listener would imply that the information is nothing new to the listener and thus of low relevance. Too much inferencing on the part of the listener would only confuse the listener. Thus the speaker must gauge his contribution to produce the optimal effect on the inferencing capacity of his listeners.

Key to eliciting the optimal amount of inferencing from the listener and to binding listeners to the speaker is to effectively reveal the speaker's intentions and meanings to the listeners. The speaker must be able to generate a string of words that conveys his or her intention and meaning in an optimal manner and a listener/recipient of the speech must be able to infer the speaker's intention from the resulting string of words. Speaker meaning is not the same as sentence meaning (or the abstract meaning of a sentence in isolation); interlocutors must go beyond sentence meaning to produce and comprehend speaker meaning (Clark, 1985; Bara, Tirassa, and Zettin, 1997; Sperber and Wilson, 1995). Speaker meaning encompasses several subcomponents. Most central perhaps to the leader-follower relation is the notion of speech acts. Speech act theory (Austin, 1962; Searle, 1969) has been a very influential approach to language use and has a richly-developed research base in the areas of analytic philosophy and logic (Grice, 1989; Searle and Vanderveken, 1985), artificial intelligence (Cohen and Levesque, 1990), psychology (Clark, 1996; Gibbs, 1999), and computational linguistics (Cohen, Morgan, and Pollack, 1990).

A speech act is the basic language tool of the leader. A speech act is the action performed just by saying the right words. For example, if the right person says the following words in the right context "I now pronounce you man and wife" that utterance has the force of making the two concerned individuals man and wife. Many types of actions can be performed simply by saying the appropriate words. If you say, "I promise..." you bind yourself to a given course of action. If you say "Open the window." You are ordering someone to do something (in this case open the window). Most language expressions are influenced by speech acts. Declaratives (I declare that... I resign..." I accept....) announce one's status or intention etc Representatives (I believe that...I represent that...I hypothesize...) declare the speakers beliefs. Commissives (I promise...I vow...I volunteer...I refuse...) commit the speaker to some future action. Directives (I command...I request...I order...I forbid...) get the listener to perform some act. Expressives (I deplore...I regret...I apologize...) express the state of mind of the speaker.

Speech acts are important for the leader as they effectively reveal the speaker's intentions and meanings. They point to the act that is most relevant to the speech/utterance/conversation. This does not mean that they point directly to the relevant intention concerning the connected act. Speech acts can also point indirectly to the intended meaning and relevant action if the indirect reference is more effective in revealing the speaker's intentions in the conversational context. The 'pointing' of the speech at to the relevant action is called illocutionary force.

Illocutionary force as defined by speech act theorists (e.g., Searle, 1969), is the action (e.g., thank, apologize, promise, etc.) a speaker intends to have recognized with an utterance. For example, when Bob says to Andy "I'll definitely do it tomorrow" he would generally be regarded as having performed the act of promising. Note that illocutionary force is often conveyed without use of the relevant speech act verb (e.g., the verb promise is not part of "I will definitely do it tomorrow"). Thus the listener MUST perform an inference to arrive at the speaker's real meaning. The speaker's utterance implies a promise. It is in this way that illocutionary force often represents a (generalized) implicature. Speech acts therefore are ideal tools for individuals who want to appear to be acting according to the relevance criterion in any given conversation. They forcefully reveal intentions/meanings by pointing to the relevant action that needs to be performed or was performed etc When indirect, they do this by having the listener perform the necessary number of inferences, not too many and not too few, to arrive at the intended meaning.

In summary then, the relevance criterion imposes strong constraints on the very structure of language itself. It says that messages must convey an optimal amount of information if they are to satisfy the relevance constraint. To do so language displays structure dependence such that the basic units of a language are the information packets we call sentences. Each sentence uses thematic roles or slots to reveal who did what to whom. This is the kind of information that a social species like us would find so valuable—so relevant. At some point in the emergence of anatomically modern humans relevance became linked with prestige. That link both facilitated the rise of 'leaders' or individuals other people would defer to, and shaped the evolution of the language faculty itself. The link between relevance and prestige was formalized by the ancients in the form of rules of rhetoric or eloquence. The rules show you how to use the tools of language to tell stories and convey information in such a way that listener's believe that they are the beneficiaries of an altruistic act performed by the speaker. As literacy became more widespread public use of rhetoric in the form of orations and story-telling was supplemented to some extent with the written word. Leaders have to become proficient at both public speech and the written word. The link between relevant speech and prestige is stronger than ever and every leader must become proficient at use of language.

We realize that our review of the components of the make up of the leader to this point has touched mainly on those traits, experiences, and manners of operating that are conducive to prestige-based leadership. We have looked at how education and intelligence contribute to the formation of a leader. We also put forth a theory regarding the way in which a good character and a sterling reputation pick out a potential leader and which, in turn, attracts followers. And we have looked at the use of rhetoric as a tool --a very important tool-- in the enlistment of followers in the quest for the leader's vision. Now we must balance our assessment of successful leaders by examining the role of dominance relations in successful leadership.

Chapter 6

THE CO-EVOLUTION OF WAR AND THE DOMINANCE STRATEGY IN LEADERSHIP

INTRODUCTION

We have argued throughout our exposition of evolutionary approaches to leadership that leaders evolved two fundamental strategies to lead people: prestige and dominance. We have emphasized that dominance need not involve brute force, but rather than it can involve subtle political and legal manipulations as well. The dominance oriented leader is the leader who attempts to become the master strategist when dealing with and manipulating opponents. He is interested in defeating or neutralizing the political power of his opponents. He wants to coerce his opponents into doing his will. What are the evolutionary roots of dominance? Part of those roots likely involved the normal everyday social interactions in human groups. These everyday social interactions can involve a lot of manipulation, deception and outright coercion. Another source, a very important and potent force, may have been war.

BIOLOGICAL CORRELATES OF DOMINANCE

In our closest animal cousins, the great apes, dominant individuals get preferential access to fertile mates, to plentiful food and space and a disproportionate amount of grooming (to reduce parasite load) from others. In short, dominance leads to enhanced reproductive fitness (Cowlishaw and Dunbar, 1991; Ellis, 1995). Women regard men who *look* dominant as attractive (Townsend, 1993). Teenage men rated by naïve judges as having "dominant looking" faces (often with prominent chins, heavy brow ridges, muscular rather than fleshy or skinny faces) report copulating earlier than their submissive-looking peers, presumably because they have an easier time recruiting partners.

Like all primates, humans in face-to-face groups form themselves into fairly consistent dominance/status hierarchies so that higher-ranked members have more power, influence, and valued prerogatives than lower-ranked ones (Mazur, 1973). Dominance hierarchies represent a kind of order within primate societies and the dominant male and his allies are expected to maintain order in the troop. There is even some indication that the dominant male needs to lead the group to plentiful food sources or some other valued resource if he is to maintain his status.

How do the hierarchies get established? Nonhuman primates do it through force, threat or outright violence. Males who want to establish their dominance must do so in agonistic encounters of one kind or another, including outright combat. Often however a series of short face-to-face competitions between members of the troop soon establishes who is dominant and who is deferential and submissive. These face to face encounters can range from a simple encounter such a stare by the powerful animal, followed by the fearful animal's eye aversion or by its yielding something of value (perhaps food or a sitting place), to violent combat between two large males wherein one is seriously injured or even killed. In short, primates can establish their dominance hierarchies through force or through the threat of force.

Rodents and many other animals seemed more tied to use of force to establish dominance than are the primates. Interestingly, dominance contests in rodents are typically accompanied by rising testosterone (abbreviated T) levels. The rising T in turn is correlated with increasing aggressiveness (Monaghan and Glickman, 1992; Svare, 1983). There is a similar link between T and dominance in primates and in humans—though it gets quite complicated. Overall, there is considerable evidence from a variety of settings that in men, circulating T is correlated with dominant or aggressive behavior, and antisocial norm breaking.

In summary, non-human dominance hierarchies are tightly linked with rising T and aggression levels and tend to involve the use of force, threat or aggression to stabilize social hierarchies. Human dominance hierarchies on the other hand are less linked to threat, force or, presumably rising T levels. War and police actions may be exceptions to this more general rule. To establish order in a war or police action one needs to use force. In most human social groups, however, order is likely to be established with the help of (though not sole reliance on) status or dominance hierarchies. These dominance hierarchies have unique properties relative to the rest of the animal world. First, they are headed by a leader who very likely carries the traits of exceptional intelligence, extroverted personality disposition, intuitive and thinking behavioral styles and strong motivations to achieve a goal etc, in short a prestige-oriented leader. Second, the hierarchy is not governed by force or threat of force (except again in special situations like war or police actions). Instead the hierarchy is governed by prestige.

Is there any evidence that leaders share a trait that might reasonably be called dominance? Are leaders in fact socially dominant individuals? In a meta-analysis of 78 studies of personality attributes of leaders, Judge, Bono, Ilies, and Berhardt (2002) found that "extroversion" exhibited the strongest relationship to leadership than any of the other of the "Big Five" personality dimensions ('openness to experience', 'agreeableness', 'conscientiousness' 'emotional stability/neuroticism'). Agreeableness demonstrated the weakest relationship to leadership of any of the big five personality dimensions. The effect sizes in Judge et al's meta-analysis were reasonably large with a multiple correlation of .48 between all 5 personality dimensions and leadership. When the Myers-Briggs personality inventory is used to compare leaders with non-leaders, leaders are more likely to exhibit a profile of extroversion combined with intuitiveness and thinking behavioral styles. Research utilizing other personality inventories have identified 'optimism', 'adaptability' and 'nurturance' as important personality styles of effective leaders. Several recent studies utilizing archival, experimental and personality assessment methods have identified a small set of motivational constructs that both predict leadership emergence and mediate effects of more global cognitive and personality factors on leadership emergence and effectiveness. These studies of motivational antecedents of leadership identify need for power, achievement and dominance as powerful motivations that differentiate leaders from non-leaders (who do not evidence any such motives on their test scores or performance profiles).

One set of traits that illustrate the personality trait related to what we are calling 'dominance' in leaders is what has been called 'social potency'. Social potency is "the self-perceived ability to influence, lead, or dominate others" (Lykken, 1982, p. 370). Monozygotic twins, whether reared apart or together, obtain significantly similar scores on social potency (a Pearson r of .67) when compared to dizygotic twins (r=.07) who are no more alike on this trait than any two people selected randomly from the population. Lykken noted that social potency is thus more than just polygenic; it may also require all the corresponding genes to participate if the trait is to appear at all. In particular, Social Potency "probably depends on some configuration of attractiveness, self-confidence, assertiveness, dominance—whatever the ingredients are of 'charisma' " (p. 370). If one component is lacking, Social Potency cannot emerge as a character trait.

Whether called social potency or dominance, we have seen that the evolutionary roots of this aspect of leadership lies at least in part in the need to suppress and punish free-riders and exploiters of the group. No trust between people and no small or large scale cooperation is possible among people unless the malign influence of the free rider can be neutralized. Leaders took on a major part of the responsibility to punish the free-rider and that is why followers consented to turning power over to the leaders. The leaders therefore had to show that they could effectively punish free-riders and enemies in general. They also had to show that they could protect and expand the resources of the group. It was these sort of imperatives that led to the leader-related dominance strategy in early human groups. We emphasize that the dominance strategy did not develop in isolation of the prestige-oriented strategy. They likely co-evolved in important ways. They are nevertheless distinct. They were to a significant extent influenced and shaped by separate evolutionary forces. In this chapter we show that the dominance strategy was decisively influenced by the evolution of war.

Even a casual acquaintance with the biographies of 'Plutarch's Lives" reveals a preponderance of military leaders. Caesar, Alexander, Pompey, Marius, Pyrrhus, Antony, Alcibiades, and several others all attained prominence through their military exploits. Even the great political leaders of the ancient world such as Pericles and Themistocles (though not so much Cicero and Cato the younger) had had serious experience as military commanders and may even be considered brilliant military tacticians. The victory of the naval battle at Salamis between the Athenian and the Persian fleets, for example, is surely due to Themistocles' brilliant tactics.

Commanding men in battle necessarily requires very considerable leadership skills. In this chapter we consider the extent to which leadership has been influenced by war. In particular we consider the extent to which the leader's ability to politically dominate his rivals and enemies and to impose order on otherwise chaotic social situations has influenced the nature and functions of leadership in human history and in contemporaneous politics. We will argue an unpopular claim: that the human psyche has been shaped and influenced by war. This is NOT to say that we are inherently killers. Instead we will argue what we believe to be obvious; that we all possess the capacity to kill on a grand scale when given the right cultural conditions. Our contribution here will be to provide a new explanation for this otherwise well-known murderous capacity all human beings possess.

First it has to be recognized that the human species co-evolved along with the evolution of warfare between early human populations. Because of this co-evolution between warfare and humanity some evolutionary psychologists have argued that the human brain and human nature itself were influenced by the evolution of warfare. To win at battle, a commander had to have a quick strategic intelligence, had to anticipate his enemies' moves—even his enemies' thoughts. He had to be able to master panic spreading among his soldiers, to endure hardship and most importantly earn the respect of his men. The commanders' 'mindreading abilities' planning abilities, foresight, and courage could spell the difference between victory and defeat, life and death for himself and his men. War, therefore, acts as an extreme agent of natural selection: only the successful warriors pass their genes down through the generations. Only the most intelligent win and pass their genes to the next generation and thus warfare very likely contributed to the evolution of the large human brain—or so the argument goes.

Did leadership co-evolve with warfare? Did the human brain itself, did intelligence, emerge from the necessities of warfare? Plutarch seems to suggest that the answer is Yes. Plutarch, however, argued that warfare could produce both excellent and poor leaders with the poor leaders often engaging in colossal stupidities (e.g., Crassus).

Crassus, the wealthy Roman aristocrat and general of the first century BC, for example, initiated an unnecessary and un-called-for war in Parthia. Out of envy of Pompey and Caesar, he desired to excel all, and thus brought Roman legions into a war they could not win. In the process he lost his son, all his hopes for greatness, and plunged the vaunted Roman legions into one of their most humiliating defeats.

In short, Crassus produced a disastrous war and caused the annihilation of an entire Roman army. But, this is just the point, say the advocates of the warfare theory of the evolution of human nature: warfare culls the stupid ones from the population. Crassus' armies did not pass their genes onto the next generation as they were all killed. Thus, genes associated with stupidity in war are culled from the population. Only the smart armies live long enough to mate and to pass their genes down the generations. Over time, therefore, the average level of human intelligence increases. That is why the instruments of warfare increase in effectiveness and lethality. To be a winning army you need to outwit and outmaneuver your enemies, who have the latest technically advanced weaponry.

In short, war evolves just as prey-predator populations evolve: The 'prey' get more clever at evading the attacks of the 'predator' and so the predator must increase the stealth and the lethality of his attacks if he is to get his prey. While the basic relationship of attack-defense-evasion etc remain the same, the sophistication of the attack and the cleverness of the evasive attacks increase over time. These predator/prey relationships therefore sometimes slowly, sometimes quickly cull the dullest specimens from the population leaving only the clever who engage in a never-ending arms race against one another. The arms race, in turn, forces an increase in the overall level of intelligence in the belligerent parties. What effects do these evolutionary dynamics have on the evolution of the traits of leaders?

Battles, of necessity, create leaders that are flexible, strategic and creative and thus battles, in general, create excellent leaders and eliminate poor leaders. One of Plutarch's apparent goals in his Lives was to analyze the contribution of warfare to the creation or to the undoing of potential leaders. Plutarch understood how battle could force a potential leader to learn quickly and to become a real leader. Take, for example, Caesar's extraordinary feats during the Gallic wars.

During these wars, Caesar very shrewdly used the prestige-oriented leadership skill of *rhetoric* to shore up support back in Rome for his Gallic military campaigns. This was important not only for his personal reputation but also for ensuring a steady supply of goods and resources for his troops. Every great general must solve this political problem or the logistical problem of keeping his troops well-fed and supplied cannot be solved. Caesar used rhetoric and political skill to do this.

He composed what became a literary masterpiece, called the 'Commentaries' or the 'Gallic Wars', which served to solidify his reputation in Rome as a first class General and conqueror. The Commentaries were written essentially as dispatches sent back to Rome at regular intervals in order to spread news of his great victories. One would think therefore that they were mere propaganda in the modern sense designed to glorify Caesar by exaggerating his accomplishments and conquests. Historians, however, have found that the dispatches contained 'matter of fact' accounts of battles that were largely accurate and without exaggeration. Caesar, in fact, had no interest in spreading lies about his actions and accomplishments. It would have been nearly impossible, in any case, to do so given the number of people involved that regularly moved between Caesar's armies in Gaul and the home base back in Rome.

Caesar's tactics in the Gallic wars varied from appalling acts of brutality and near genocide to the occasional act of generosity in victory. After he defeated the migrating Helvetii, for example, (and he did this by tricking the Helvetii into premature battle), he allowed survivors and their families to return to their homelands and even gave them provisions. Nevertheless he relied for the most part on harsh and brutal treatment of opposing armies in order to spread terror and fear of the Roman armies. To facilitate the systematic subjugation of the Celtic tribes of Gaul, Caesar developed very subtle diplomatic techniques to prevent the tribes from uniting in opposition to Rome. Thus, he could deal separately with each of the major tribes defeating them one by one.

In 57 BC Caesar defeated the Nervii—the fiercest of the Belgae tribes. In 56 BC, he followed up this success by defeating the coastal tribes of the Venetii. Here he had to train some of his soldiers to become sailors. Caesar devised a simple technique to disable the ships of the Venetii. He used javelin-like devices to puncture the sails and cut the ropes of the enemy ships thus leaving them dead and vulnerable in the water as they did not use rowers.

In 55BC Caesar invaded Britain and somewhat recklessly did not put enough planning into beaching his ships safely. They were thus destroyed on the beaches by the weather, the ocean and by enemy armies. This is one of the many instances in which his phenomenal speed when in attack mode put him at risk. Typically his speed surprised the enemy and gave the initiative to Caesar but occasionally his own supply lines and troops had trouble keeping up with him. As legend put it, Caesar's military strikes were often delivered too soon but none were delivered too late.

With his ships in tatters on the beaches of Dover, he now had no means of escape. Instead of panicking, however, he simply built some fortifications, dragged what remained of the ships behind these fortifications and had his engineers repair as many as they could while sending for reinforcements back to the mainland of Gaul. This is a prime leadership skill for leaders facing crisis situations (i.e. eventually all leaders).

The ability to stay calm and focused and to think clearly in times of crisis, in short, *to not panic* when all around you are panicking is crucial for leadership success in any kind of endeavor.

While the British campaign did little to establish a Roman presence in Britain, it certainly impressed the people back home in Rome because Britain was largely 'terra incognita'. Britain was at the limits of the known world for Romans. When he returned from the British campaign he faced a rebellion of virtually all of the Celtic tribes. His policies of harsh treatment of the defeated tribes came back to haunt the Roman armies eventually causing virtually all of the Gallic tribes to unite under a single and able leader, Vercingetorix.

Vercingetorix was only twenty years old when the rebellion began to take fire. He was strongly supported, however, by the Druids, the Celtic priests and the Celtic peoples therefore rallied round him. Within months Vercingetorix had raised over 80,000 troops eager to take on Caesar. He recommended a scorched earth policy to his countrymen in order to deny Caesar's armies the provisions necessary to conduct war. This policy was religiously adhered to by most of the Celtic peoples and Caesar's men almost starved to death. Nevertheless, Caesar finally caught up with Vercingetorix's armies near Gergovia. Here Caesar used one of his favorite stratagems on Vercingetorix: he first attacked the Celtic armies prematurely and was repulsed. The Celtic armies believed this to be a victory but Vercingetorix himself, knew it to be only a probe. Caesar then pretended to undertake a strategic retreat from the field thus luring the Celtic armies into a vulnerable position between Caesar's flanks. Even with Vercingetorix's superior numbers the battle was not decided until Caesar's German cavalry entered the battle, defeated Vercingetorix's cavalry and forced a retreat of the Celtic armies. Vercingetorix was forced off the field and retreated behind fortifications at the city of Alesia in 52 BC

This retreat was sound strategy on Vercingetorix's part because he knew he had reinforcements on the way. Indeed, a force of approximately 250,000 Gallic warriors were headed to relieve Alesia. Caesar had at most 50,000 men. When news of the massing of hostile reinforcements reached Caesar's camps, his soldiers started to panic as it was clear they were going to be surrounded and thus likely annihilated. While most other generals would have fled, Caesar once again *did not panic*. He acted quickly and decisively. Indeed he went on the offensive. He constructed siege works that steadily threatened the city walls and prevented supplies from reaching the city. But he also shored up his defenses. In order to protect his rear, he built a series of trenches between his camps and the approaching relieving force such that his men could now face the enemy behind fortifications no matter which way they faced.

When the relief force arrived Caesar's armies found themselves under attack for 4 straight days and from all sides. Caesar's lines however never gave way and when he finally saw signs of flagging in the Celtic attack waves Caesar sent his German cavalry out from behind his fortifications and into the rear of the relieving forces thus throwing these forces into disarray. This demoralized the warriors and when their leaders later proved incapable of restoring morale or even of supplying them with food the relieving armies started to melt away. Vercingetorix, starving within the city, finally decided to surrender and Caesar shipped him back to Rome to imprisonment and ultimate execution. Thus ended the Gallic Wars.

By the end of the Gallic wars Caesar had reduced all of Gaul to Roman control. In the course of the Gallic campaigns Caesar had fought at least 30 major battles, winning virtually all of them. He captured over 800 towns, over a million enemy soldiers and killed another million. He conquered an area twice the size of Italy itself with far more millions of people than the province of Spain. What is more is that the lands were largely fertile and the towns potentially rich. Caesar's conquests turned the Roman empire into a world-wide land empire rather than just a Mediterranean phenomenon. These Gallic campaigns proved him one of the greatest military commanders of all time.

The example of Caesar and the testimonies of the rest of the lives told in Plutarch's biographies testify to the tight relationship between military skill and leadership in the ancient world. Indeed, it would be no exaggeration to claim that war has been the crucible through which male leadership skills have been honed down through the centuries. We are NOT claiming however, that war was the only influence on development of male leadership skills/styles—only that it had a significant and lasting impact.

It is also important to note that a thesis that leadership skills in the male co-evolved with the evolution of warfare DOES NOT entail that male leadership profiles will always involve top-down authoritarian command type leadership styles. *It is very probable that war stimulates the capacity for cooperation as well as conflict.* Paradoxically, in order to win at war you and your group need to learn how to cooperate among yourselves. Dissension within your own ranks invariably leads to defeat.

Look at the leadership decisions of Lucullus for example. Lucullus was a brilliant military leader, but he failed to rally the political support that he needed domestically to build a lasting and prosperous Roman state. Perhaps he failed to grasp how Roman military and civic life were changing as Roman territory expanded. For centuries Roman leaders had followed a similar career. Military success won the opportunity to return to Rome for a triumph, election to an office of honor and responsibility, with consul being the highest office, then entrance into the senate to take one's place among the respected and powerful governors of the republic. It was a pattern that worked well as long as Rome's enemies were nearby, as in the early years when she was subjugating the surrounding cities of Italy, and even when conquering the Gauls in northern Italy and nearer parts of Europe. Citizen-soldiers would take up arms in the summer campaign season and return in time for the harvest. Military commanders were never long away from the city and the military and civic functions of government were never far apart. But this was changing. Rome's enemies were farther away and campaigns could no longer be concluded in a season. A generation earlier Marius, in 107 BC reorganized the army by enlisting slaves and poor people, thus changing the character of the army from a citizen to professional army (Life of Marius, 9). The great military exploits of Lucullus were done during his long absences from Rome, during which time other men, not necessarily as talented as Lucullus at commanding an army, but with the advantage of being in Rome where they could sway the crowd and argue in the senate, held office and with envious eye regarded Lucullus' Asian exploits as a threat to their own careers rather than a credit to Rome.

Lucullus, perhaps, just didn't understand the need to run a campaign of political rhetoric at home while campaigning against Rome's enemies abroad. Thus Lucullus allowed dissension within his own ranks to develop. His own base, the Roman citizenry, turned against him and he fell. The next generation of leaders, Pompey the Great, Julius Caesar, and finally, Octavian known as Augustus demonstrated an ever increasing awareness of shoring up the base and cultivating this vital blending of the military and the civic virtues. War leaders therefore are also virtuoso peacemakers—at least within their own ranks/group.

Let us now look at some evolutionary psychology approaches to war to see if they can teach us anything about the nature of the dominance strategy of leadership.

Despite the overall increase in the lethality of weapons and the sophistication of strategy and tactics, war still appears to be a grand display of folly, stupidity and waste. War uses the best and brightest, who produce the most lethal weapons known to mankind as well as the best strategic scenarios and battlefield tactics, all in the service of a colossal waste of life and treasure. Why?

One possibility is that war is not a waste. The victors gain substantial reproductive advantages over enemies. But this has not been even remotely demonstrated and it is difficult to see how it could be demonstrated. On the face of is it seems simple: we kill all your defenders and then take your resources including your treasure and your women. Therefore we are better off from a reproductive point of view. Our genes are more likely to be passed to future generations of the human race.

Unfortunately for this simple scenario whatever benefits are gained are transient and short lived if they are real at all. Wars are so frequent in human history that it is crystal clear that no one group stays on top for long. In addition, if the victors mate with the women of the opposing group then genes associated with the enemy will continue to be propagated along with the victor's genes. In addition, it is not at all clear that war's putative genetic benefits outweigh its genetic costs. Could a group better propagate its genes through cooperative or more peaceful means than via war? No one has yet adequately addressed this elementary question.

Thus, the jury is out on the question of whether war functions to facilitate gene transmission of the victors.

Another explanation of the ubiquity of war in human populations is therefore required. In the evolutionary psychology literature 'war', from its most primitive incarnations to its most advanced forms, falls under a very unusual form of aggressive behavior known as coalitional aggression. What is unusual about coalitional aggression is that only 2, maybe 3, species practice it. These are the very intelligent humans, chimpanzees and perhaps dolphins. In the most intelligent of these species, humans, coalitional aggression led directly to war.

Coalitional aggression (i.e., raiding and warfare) evolved, according to Tooby and Cosmides (1988), because it allowed participants in such coalitions, typically composed of males, to promote their reproductive fitness by gaining access to greater than usual numbers of young fertile females. Among preindustrial societies, ambush warfare by raiding parties of varying size (almost indistinguishable from ambushes by male chimpanzees), appears to have been the common pattern. The rewards, as in the individual or communal fighting of other species, were reproductive: Women as mates, and resources to purchase women as mates.

In a typical act of coalitional aggression, males of one group band together to attack the males of another group in order to kidnap their fertile females. It apparently requires exceptional cognitive abilities to do this…as no other species besides the 3 just mentioned engage in the practice. Clearly the most salient characteristic the three share is a large brain.

But where does the requirement for intelligence come in? It takes a very specialized form of intelligence to solve the problem of coordinating attacks on intelligent conspecifics without getting killed or injured. These coordination problems boil down once again to the problem of cooperation and social exchange—problems we have discussed at length in previous chapters. War, more than any other social enterprise requires very sophisticated forms of cooperation if it is to succeed. The requirement to learn cooperation in turn places heavy demands on cognitive abilities.

As mentioned above war acts as an agent of natural selection selecting only those individuals strong enough and intelligent not to get killed in battle. Those individuals who did not have the requisite savvy during battle obviously got killed off…and their genes did not get passed down the generations. Thus war provides a kind of ratcheting effect in terms of the evolution of intelligence: the greater demands it places on planning, cooperation, stealth, deception, courage, control of panic, management of supply trains and leadership etc, the more efficiently does it promote the rise of intelligence. The greater the intelligence of the opposing war bands, in turn, requires yet greater levels of inventiveness in the members of each team in order to win battles and so forth.

Tooby and Cosmides propose that humans have evolved specialized *Darwinian algorithms*, or innate cognitive programs, that govern coalitional behavior, and which constitute a distinctive coalitional psychology. A most salient aspect of this coalitional psychology is in-group *Cooperation*, and out-group hostility.

Most animals when they are conspecifics (members of the same species) engage in fights or bouts of aggressive displays and attacks between two individuals. No cooperative behavior is required. A war, on the other hand, is an aggressive conflict between two *coalitions*, and would not be possible unless each coalition were able to sustain itself as a group of cooperating individuals.

We reviewed in previous chapters recent theoretical and empirical advances in evolutionary biology and game theory approaches to the evolution of cooperation (Axelrod, 1984: Axelrod and Hamilton, 1981; Maynard-Smith, 1982; Trivers, 1971). That work has shown that, if cooperation (independent of kin selection) is to evolve and function stably, it must satisfy the following conditions:

1. Social or ecological conditions must create frequent and recurrent situations where there are enhanced payoffs to cooperation.
2. Cooperators must be able to identify free-riders
3. Cooperators must be able to exclude or punish free-riders

These simple principles very accurately explain why and how cooperation evolves among animal species. It evolves because it provides pay-offs or benefits to cooperators and it excludes benefits accruing to free-riders. We have seen in previous chapters that in the context of human evolution, the leader likely played a major role in facilitating the evolution of cooperation. That is because the leader found a way (development of costly to maintain character strengths) to exclude free-riders without active punishment etc. All that cooperators needed to do was to develop character strengths such as reliability, integrity, intelligence etc and inhibition of exploitative free-rider behavioral impulses. Development of these character strengths in turn, would actively weed out the free-riders because free-riders would not be willing to inhibit exploitative behavioral strategies for long periods of time. Nor would they be willing to develop the costly character strengths just mentioned—all of which are inimical to exploitative behavioral strategies.

The need to punish free-riders however required powerful individuals who could enforce penalties on uncooperative individuals. The leaders became the enforcers. But enforcement procedures could very easily blend into coalitional aggression against neighboring tribes instead of free-riders within the tribe itself. It is likely then that the emergence of leaders also facilitated the evolution of coalitional aggression in humans. It may be that the distribution of war in the animal kingdom to humans and chimpanzees (and perhaps to bottlenose dolphins) is limited by the same factor (intelligent control of the free-rider) that limits the emergence of the multi-individual cooperation on which war depends. Only humans and chimpanzees have the necessary brain-power to inhibit free-rider behavioral strategies over long periods of time. The cognitive prerequisites necessary to exclude cheaters from benefiting from joint action as much as, or more than, genuine cooperators must involve at a minimum rapid identification of potential cheats; rapid development of a strategy to exclude these cheats or rapid development of the resources necessary to punish cheats. The difference between chimps and humans appears to be that humans used leaders and their exceptional character strengths to exclude free-riders while chimps rely more on brute force to punish free-riders.

If we place ourselves back into early human evolutionary history at the dawn of the age of the emergence of coalitional aggression in the form of raids on neighboring groups/tribes we can ask ourselves what the appearance of the leader might have meant for the rise of this early form of warfare. What does a leader need to consider when considering a potential battle? In calculating the elements that factor into a model of the psychology of coalitional aggression (and later war) the leader would want to include: the risk to himself and to each of his followers, strategy and tactics, the probability of achieving success, the payoff if his coalition wins, and how to allocate the spoils to each of his followers.

Looked at from the level of the group benefits, , the deaths of some members of a coalition during a war will not decrease the *average* fitness of the members of the coalition, because the reproductive opportunities within the coalition, or gained as the result of victory, will simply accrue to the survivors. While it is true that each individual who dies loses, each survivor, on the other hand, gains to the same extent. Provided the participants do not know *in advance* who will live and who will die, cooperation will be possible in the coalition and the group decision to go to war will benefit its members.

As noted above, the emergence of coalitional aggression requires enforcement of the risk contract—i.e. that risk of death and injury be roughly equivalent across members of the coalition. Once again free-riders will attempt to escape any risk to themselves and thus enforcement of the risk contract boils down to handling the problem of the free-rider. Once again we see that the evolution of cooperation, in this case cooperation in war, requires that an individual will emerge who has the power to enforce and to identify and punish free-riders. That individual will become a leader.

It is crucial to point out that in Tooby and Cosmides' model of the evolution of coalitional aggression it was mostly men fighting each other over access to females rather than to food resources. A group of men would benefit from initiating a battle to claim new women only if they were flush with food and other resources. Then they would know that their existing mates and offspring could survive without them. In evolutionary terms, they don't lose much by going to war for women even if many were to die, their offspring would survive to pass on their genes. And if the group won and gained new mates, the male coalition would bear more young on average, even if a few men lost their lives in the effort...

In sum, the benefits of warfare to males in preindustrial societies include increased direct access to reproductive females, and increased material resources useful for the lineage. Coalitional aggression benefited groups engaging in war and forced both attackers and defenders over time to increase intra-group cooperative abilities and inter-group hostility. Warfare also forced both attackers and defenders to increase their skills and overall level of intelligence. Because coalitional violence required very high levels of intra-group cooperation it had to solve the problem of the free-rider (discussed in previous chapters). Once again part of the solution to that problem involved the emergence of leaders who had the authority and resources to identify and punish free-riders. The leader also functioned as commander in the battles themselves and these battles in turn shaped the skill-set and skill-levels of the leaders. Leaders had to become more strategic, cunning, deceptive, inspirational and audacious in their leadership styles if they were to win battles. In short, war was shaped by the leader and the leader was shaped by war.

Chapter 7

PRESTIGE-ORIENTED VERSUS DOMINANCE-ORIENTED STYLES OF LEADERSHIP

We have seen in previous chapters how leaders in early human groups became distinguished from the crowd—how in fact they were 'elected' into leadership roles. They distinguished themselves in two major respects: they followed the prestige option or the domination option. Presumably there were some leaders who combined the two options in various ways and these latter leaders, enshrined in myth, were very likely the most memorable. Flexibility is certainly a mark of a great leader.

Leaders who relied on the prestige option had to emphasize matters of character, of integrity and of virtue. They had to use language and rhetoric well. Integrity of character and the fluent use of language indicated altruistic intent. Only someone who could exhibit sterling character virtues such as trustworthiness, generosity and self-sacrifice would be able and willing to forego selfish short term rewards for longer term goals. Similarly when someone uses language to deliver valuable information to followers (the principle of relevance) it is an altruistic act because it immediately benefits followers at some cost to the speaker. Thus, *character strengths* and *effective rhetoric* mark out the prestige-oriented leader from both the dominance –oriented leader and the mass of followers.

Leaders who relied on the dominance-oriented option also had to exhibit a quick wit, a strategic mind, physical prowess and high intelligence. Because the dominance oriented leader is interested primarily in coercing opponents and followers he needs to become a master political operative and manipulator. Finally when all else fails in the manipulation repertoire the dominance oriented leader will resort to outright force to achieve his aims.

We turn now to a discussion of the major differences between the prestige and the dominance options and the ways in which a flexible leader can use the two strategies 'facultatively' according to the contextual demands of the political situation he faces. After elucidation of the major differences between the two leadership styles we emphasize the fact that both are needed to create really effective leadership. When one option is relied upon too exclusively aberrations in leadership abound. The leader who, for example, relies solely on persuasion and prestige will inevitably become weak and ineffective. The leader who, on the other hand relies solely on the dominance and manipulation option will become arbitrary and abusive, leading to loss of the support of his followers, rendering him ineffective.

PRESTIGE VS. DOMINANCE

What we are calling the dominance option here shares some similarities with the dynamics of non-human primate dominance hierarchies while the prestige option shares some similarities with human social hierarchies. Henrich and Gil-White (2001) have summarized many of the biologic differences between non-human primate and human hierarchical social orders. Non-human primate dominance hierarchies are established via force or threat of force. Every relationship is predominantly transitive and asymmetric with little give and take or reciprocal altruism. Low status individuals are not allowed to approach dominant individuals without cost. Nor are they allowed to stare at high status individuals without cost. High status individuals may attack lower status individuals especially if a low status individual challenges a higher status individual. High status individuals are frequently imitated by lower status individuals and may even under special circumstances be groomed by lower status individuals. The behavioral disposition of high status individuals among non-human primates involves a kind of very noticeable swagger that serves to intimidate and instill fear in all who observe the swagger. Something like this swagger is observed in human societies though it must be said to be muted. The only ethological characteristic that the non-human primate dominance hierarchy has in common with the human prestige hierarchy is that the high status individuals receive an abundance of favors, resources, gifts and services from low status individuals (see Table 1, modeled after Henrich and Gil-White, 2001, p. 171).

**Table 1. Ethological Differences between dominance
and prestige organized social hierarchies**

	Dominance Hierarchy	Prestige Hierarchy
Orders	Some non-human primates (excluding perhaps Bonobos)	Humans
Hierarchy and order established by force?	yes	Only in special situations like war and police actions
Low status individual approaches high status individual without cost?	no	yes
Low status individual stares at high status individual without cost?	no	yes
Social mobility established via attack: low status individual attack high status individuals?	yes	No except perhaps in war
Low status individual fears high status individual?	yes	Maybe (when high status individuals control resources of low status individual
High status individual can violently attack low status individual?	yes	No

Table 1 (continued)

	Dominance Hierarchy	Prestige Hierarchy
Social emulation: High status individual is imitated by low status individuals?	no	yes
High status individual 'swaggers'?	Yes, indiscriminately	Selectively
High status individual receives gifts /service from low status individuals?	yes	yes
Social relations?	Transitive and asymmetric	Reciprocal altruism

PRESTIGE AND THE EVOLUTIONARY ORIGINS OF LEADERSHIP

In short, prestige is central to the evolution of social order in human societies. Individuals who gain prestige are in a position to become leaders. Status confers prestige but the factor that makes high status individuals into leaders is social learning. Some individuals with high status and high prestige are copied or imitated by others and it is these individuals who are considered leaders.

In previous chapters, we have seen that prestige fundamentally derives from what has been called "information and resource holding potential". Individuals who can convince others that they know something important or have access to something important will automatically be given deferential treatment. If opportunity arises for observation of the high status individual over a period of time such that the low status individual gains an opportunity to establish the reliability of the high status individual's "information", then the high status individual will potentially be imitated. One of the crucial factors that will confer prestige on an individual is the ability of that individual to convince others that he or she has something important to share. As the capacity for language-based communication evolved in humans good story telling abilities and what would later become known as rhetoric became prime signals of information holding capacity and thus of prestige. A tribal leader who could give a good speech before the tribal assembly was given deference in tribal councils and so forth. Good story telling abilities later evolved into more formalized methods of persuasion called rhetoric which we discussed in a previous chapter.

Rhetoric was studied and formalized by leaders in the ancient world because it worked-it helped the leader to energize, train and lead followers to places where the leader wanted to take them. All of the ancient texts on rhetoric emphasize that the one ingredient that could not be learned from the manuals or the trivium was how to develop a high moral character. Character, in turn, was important, as no amount of persuasive speech would work without some certification of the character of the individual delivering the speech. Reputation and prestige were all important to the ancient leader.

Human's special abilities at social learning, social imitation and emulation of high status individuals who have earned their prestige due to effective use of rhetoric and to high 'information holding potential' suggests that the evolution of prestige-oriented leadership was determined by a process of gene-culture evolution. While genes encode basic capacities for intelligence and personality (extroversion and need for achievement etc), the social environment determines, in interaction with innate talents and intelligence, an individuals' opportunities for attaining high status and prestige. Once prestige is attained, social emulation of the prestigious individual follows and then the individual is poised for becoming a leader. The leader's prestige would have to be backed up with consistent and reliable 'delivery of the goods'. The desire on behalf of followers to identify true leaders would tend to work for stable status hierarchies as low status individuals would need to observe potential leaders over time to establish that they could consistently deliver the goods. Once reliability was established all of the usual signals of dominance would be triggered: the high status individual would receive deference, resources and services from low status individuals. Most importantly the high status individual would begin to be copied by individuals aspiring to higher status. Once he sees that emulation brings him more resources (in the form of other individuals delivering goods or services to him in exchange for the information he holds), the high status individual will morph into the role of a teacher. Over time the high status individual will act as a teacher to the low status individuals gathered around him. He will teach them and they will imitate him. This teacher-student relation, or master-disciple relation as well as the emulation process itself, will become the distinguishing pathway that leads to leadership for the prestige-oriented individual.

What about the dominance –oriented individual? His path to leadership will not emphasize learning, information, character building and rhetoric and so forth. He nevertheless still needs to demonstrate 'resource holding potential' in order to get people to follow him. How then will an individual in early human groups demonstrate resource holding potential if the prestige route is foreclosed to him? He will use political manipulation and/or outright force. He may be a hunter who brings home extra meat from the hunt, or a gatherer who brings home extra medicinal herbs for the tribe. As long as he can confer some reliable benefits on his confederates, he will able to recruit a small coalition of followers, who in exchange for some benefit such as increased knowledge of the hunt, will follow this dominant individual. In order to keep his small collation in existence he will need to become adept at manipulating individuals in his coalition in order to keep them happy. He will also need to continually produce bribes in order to keep the coalition intact. Thus there will be the need for almost continual warfare.

In the modern world, of course, the dominance-oriented leader does not need war to stay in power. But he does need to bribe his followers and thus this aspect of the relation to followers distinguishes the prestige-oriented from the dominance oriented leader. The prestige oriented leader does not need to bribe his followers because they value information almost as equal to more basic resources like food and money.

Let us look at a couple of examples of the two leadership styles from the pages of Plutarch's lives.

LEADERS EMPHASIZING DOMINANCE RATHER THAN PRESTIGE

Sometimes a leader, typically a military man, fit only for transient moments of dominance on the battlefield seeks to reach for prestige beyond the battlefield but then fails miserably to the mutual ruin of himself and his followers. The story of Marc Antony (83-30

BC) is familiar to many readers from the Shakespeare plays and Hollywood movies. Early on Antony shows his soldiering skill and his imposing appearance. He displays a great natural talent for commanding men (Life of Antony, 3-4). He rises as one of Julius Caesar's most trusted, and most effective, lieutenants in the grand struggle between Caesar and Pompey as Rome breaks into two factions in 50 BC (Life of Antony, 5).

The famous funeral oration over the bloody body of Caesar, following the assassination on the Ides of March, 44 BC, is, as most readers know, the high-water mark of Antony's career.

> Friends, Romans, countrymen, lend me your ears!
> I come to bury Caesar, not to praise him.
> The evil that men do lives after them.
> The good is oft interred with their bones;
> So let it be with Caesar. The noble Brutus
> Hath told you Caesar was ambitious;
> If it were so, it was a grievous fault,
> And grievously hath Caesar answer'd it.
> Here, under leave of Brutus and the rest-
> For Brutus is an honorable man;
> So are they all, all honorable men...
> *–Shakespeare,* Julius Caesar, III, 2.

> All of which excited the people to such indignation, that they would not defer the funeral, but, making a pile of tables and forms in the very market-place, set fire to it; and everyone, taking a brand, ran to the conspirators' houses, to attack them. –Life of Antony, 14

But equally famous is Antony's precipitous downfall: his character flaw of inordinate sensuality leads to his bewitchment by Cleopatra, which in turn led inevitably to his destruction at Actium by Octavian. Is Antony then a great man or a failure?

> Antony was not long in winning the hearts of the soldiers, joining with them in their exercises, and for the most part living amongst them, and making them presents to the utmost of his abilities; but with all others he was unpopular enough. He was too lazy to pay attention to the complaints of persons who were injured; he listened impatiently to petitions; and he had an ill name for familiarity with other people's wives. In short, the government of Caesar got a bad repute through his friends. And of these friends, Antony, as he had the largest trust, and committed the greatest errors, was thought the most deeply in fault. –Life of Antony, 6

If a central task of the leader is the creation of an ordered society, then character matters, and, surely, order hardly proceeds from a man whose own life is disordered by sensuality. To return to Plutarch's narration of the life of Antony: he tells us that Antony's familiarity among the soldiers made him popular with the men; but his undisciplined and dissolute life brought both Antony and Caesar into ill repute.

> Antony...lost his favor with the common people while...his general course of life made him, as Cicero says, absolutely odious, utter disgust being excited by his drinking bouts at all hours, his wild expenses, his gross amours, the day spent in sleeping or walking off his debauches, and the night in banquets and at theaters, and in celebrating the nuptials of some

comedian or buffoon. It is related that, drinking all night...on the morning, having to harangue the people, he came forward, overcharged as he was, and vomited before them all, one of his friends holding his gown for him. –Life of Antony, 8

Caesar overlooks Antony's faults as his skills with the army are indispensable. With Antony as his best officer, Caesar defeats Pompey's army at Pharsalia, 48 BC Caesar pursues Pompey to Egypt and sends Antony to Rome with full powers to rule in his absence (Life of Antony, 7-8). When Caesar is assassinated Antony has his moment of destiny. Brutus and the conspirators flee and Antony seizes the opportunity to become chief man in Rome. Antony, Octavian, and Lepidus form the second triumvirate and set out to rule Rome. But at the moment when, as the senior member of the triumvirate, he could have achieved greatness Antony again indulges his weakness for dissolute living.

> This triumvirate was very hateful to the Romans, and Antony most of all bore the blame, because...he was no sooner settled in his affairs, but he returned to his luxurious and dissolute way of living. Besides the ill reputation he gained by his general behavior...[His house] was filled inside with players, jugglers, and drunken flatterers, upon whom were spent the greatest part of the wealth which violence and cruelty procured. --Life of Antony, 21

Antony then travels to Asia where he further indulges in sensuality with excesses that can be maintained only by imposing ruinous taxation (Life of Antony, 24). While in Cilicia in 41 BC Antony meets Cleopatra; his passion for her will be his undoing.

> Such being his temper, the last and crowning mischief that could befall him came in the love of Cleopatra, to awaken and kindle to fury passions that as yet lay still and dormant in his nature, and to stifle and finally corrupt any elements that yet made resistance in him, of goodness and a sound judgment. –Life of Antony, 25

Plutarch tells us that

> "Philotas, a physician of Amphissa, who was at that time a student of medicine in Alexandria, used to tell my grandfather Lamprias, that, having some acquaintance with one of the royal cooks, he was invited by him, being a young man, to come and see the sumptuous preparations for supper. So he was taken into the kitchen, where he admired the prodigious variety of all things; but particularly, seeing eight wild boars roasting whole, says he, "Surely you have a great number of guests." The cook laughed at his simplicity, and told him there were not above twelve to sup, but that every dish was to be served up just roasted to a turn, and if anything was but one minute ill-timed, it was spoiled; "And," said he, "maybe Antony will sup just now, maybe not this hour, maybe he will call for wine, or begin to talk, and will put it off. So that," he continued, "it is not one, but many suppers must be had in readiness, as it is impossible to guess at his hour." –Life of Antony, 28

Antony dotes on Cleopatra and puts out his legal wife Octavia, the sister of Octavian. Antony has two children, Alexander and Cleopatra, by Cleopatra. And when Antony gives Cleopatra large territories conquered by Rome, the Roman people begin to grumble. Octavian seizes on the ill treatment of his sister Octavia to quarrel with Antony. Octavian reads to the Senate, the legal will of Antony, revealing that Antony desires to be buried in Alexandria, not

Rome. That was the final outrage and Rome declares war on Cleopatra and Antony in 31 BC (Life of Antony, 36-37 and Life of Antony, 54).

Led on to his destruction by Cleopatra, Antony begins to prepare for open war with Octavian, but he allows his infatuation with Cleopatra to cloud his otherwise clear military judgment. Antony has commanding superiority in numbers of infantry and he is about matched with Octavian for cavalry; although Antony has more ships available for this engagement, Octavian has overall sea superiority. The truth is that Antony has neither the skilled sailors nor the sort of ships needed for victory. Although Antony has the land advantage over Octavian, he chooses to fight at sea to please Cleopatra. All the while Cleopatra's ship lies at some distance, ready, according to Plutarch, to flee should the battle go badly for Antony. Octavian lures Antony into open sea where, with his smaller more easily maneuvered ships, Octavian can surround Antony's fleet (Life of Antony, 60).

According to Plutarch neither side was gaining a clear advantage, when both were surprised to see Cleopatra's ships quit the scene. Antony abandons the fight and his men and follows Cleopatra. He boards Cleopatra's ship; sits in silence for three days. When Antony receives word that his forces are defeated by Octavian at the Battle of Actium, September 2, 31 BC (Life of Antony, 67-68), Antony and Cleopatra indulge in a final debauch of laugh-and-love-for-tomorrow-we die.

> Canidius now came, bringing word in person of the loss of the army before Actium. All this, however, seemed not to disturb him, but, as if he were glad to put away all hope, that with it he might be rid of all care, and leaving his habitation by the sea, which he called the Timoneum, he was received by Cleopatra in the palace, and set the whole city into a course of feasting, drinking, and presents. --Life of Antony, 71

Cleopatra locks herself in her tomb and has word sent to Antony that she is dead. Antony falls on his sword but lingers long enough to go to the tomb of Cleopatra. The dying Antony is raised by ropes to Cleopatra's tomb and dies in her arms (Life of Antony, 76). The story of Antony and Cleopatra ends with the Queen of the Nile destroying herself with fatal bite of an asp.

Plutarch tells us that Antony's children from Cleopatra and his first wife Fulvia were reared by Octavia; they intermarried with the Imperial family and produced rulers of Rome, including the disastrous Nero, who like his forefather Antony, unwilling or unable to bridle his passions, ruined himself and very nearly ruined Rome.

The life of Antony stands as a cautionary tale of the peril of not controlling the passions. Antony was blessed with many advantages. His mother Julia was of the great family of the Caesars; his grandfather Antony had been a famous orator. Indeed, Antony is credited as being descended from the legendary hero Hercules. He had no lack of mentors and must have received the classical education of a young Roman aristocrat. So what went wrong? Plutarch traces Antony's weakness to his inordinate sensuality and this to his corruption early in life via immoral associates.

> Antony grew up a very beautiful youth, but, by the worst of misfortunes, he fell into the acquaintance and friendship of Curio, a man abandoned to his pleasures; who, to make Antony's dependence upon him a matter of greater necessity, plunged him into a life of drinking and dissipation, and led him through a course of such extravagance, that he ran, at that early age, into debt to the amount of two hundred and fifty talents. For this sum, Curio

became his surety; on hearing which, the elder Curio, his father, drove Antony out of his house. After this, for some short time, he took part with Clodius, the most insolent and outrageous demagogue of the time. –Life of Antony, 2

For an Antony–good looking, rich, well-connected, successful in battle, beloved of his men–high command comes with an easy self-assurance. That can be a great asset as well as a grave threat. For such a man, unless he subdue his infantile appetites through introspection, reflection on the fleeting nature of fortune and fame, and constant striving for the good rather than the merely expedient or pleasant, will have little resource for withstanding the temptation to give in to desires and passions. Thus, as Plato said, great natures produce great vices as well as virtues (Life of Demetrius, 1).

Interestingly the moments in Antony's Life where he did best were moments under Julius Caesar's command. There are many men like Antony who cannot govern themselves but who have enough wit to allow themselves to be governed by others who have demonstrated more self-control. Once Caesar was eliminated from the scene however Antony allowed himself to be governed by Cleopatra, who however, wily and politically brilliant, was, unfortunately, no Caesar.

Another example of a dominance oriented military leader who sought extra-military honors but failed is Lucullus. Lucullus, like Antony, was a brilliant military general. He extended Rome's control over new territories and defeated kings at the height of their power. According to Plutarch,

> "Lucullus was the first Roman who carried an army over Taurus, passed the Tigris, took and burnt the royal palaces of Asia in the sight of the kings, seizing and overwhelming the northern parts as far as the Phasis, the east as far as Media, and making the South and Red Sea his own through the kings of the Arabians. He shattered the power of the kings, and narrowly missed their persons, while like wild beasts they fled away into deserts and thick and impassable woods." --Comparison of Lucullus with Cimon, 3

Lucullus was a master of varied tactics in battle. When he marches into Asia in preparation for engaging the forces of Mithridates in 74 BC, Lucullus, calculating that the large host of Mithridates will soon run out of provisions, waits for his opportunity rather than rushing into battle. He cuts the supply-lines of Mithridates. The troops of Mithridates, being famished, soon lose heart and are defeated by Lucullus (Life of Lucullus, 7-11). Later, when Lucullus faces both Mithridates and Tigranes at the battle of Tigranocerta in 69 BC, Mithridates, smarting from his early defeat at the hands of Lucullus, urges Tigranes to cut Lucullus' supply-lines rather than rashly engage the enemy, but Tigranes, not wishing to share the victory with his father-in-law Mithridates, throws himself against the Romans and is repulsed. Then Lucullus, acting exactly opposite to the way he did in the earlier battle where, greatly outnumbered, he forebear to attack, waiting rather for his enemy's food stores to give out, now goes swiftly on the defensive. Lucullus divides his forces, leaving his lieutenant Murena to press the siege of Tigranocerta, while Lucullus goes against Tigranes. Mithridates and Tigranes, thinking Lucullus will employ his customary waiting tactic are caught unawares and Lucullus, with a smaller and more lightly armed force, utterly routs the forces of Tigranes (Life of Lucullus, 26-28).

Plutarch also records that Lucullus freed the cities of the Middle East of their crippling debts and ousted their oppressors (Life of Lucullus, 20). For his labors, Lucullus created rich and powerful enemies and is seen as spending Roman resources to liberate barbarians. Back home in Rome he was criticized for pursuing a foreign war for his own glory but not to the advantage of the Roman people (Life of Lucullus, 24). He never was able to effectively answer his critics in the realm of political debate. He had not learned the liberal art of rhetoric.

Lucullus was a brilliant military leader, but he failed to rally the political support that he needed domestically to build a lasting and prosperous Roman state. Perhaps he failed to grasp how Roman military and civic life were changing as Roman territory expanded. For centuries Roman leaders had followed a similar career. Military success won the opportunity to return to Rome for a triumph, election to an office of honor and responsibility, with consul being the highest office, then entrance into the senate to take one's place among the respected and powerful governors of the republic. It was a pattern that worked well as long as Rome's enemies were nearby, as in the early years when she was subjugating the surrounding cities of Italy, and even when conquering the Gauls in northern Italy and nearer parts of Europe. Citizen-soldiers would take up arms in the summer campaign season and return in time for the harvest. Military commanders were never long away from the city and the military and civic functions of government were never far apart. But this was changing in Lucullus' time. Had Lucullus received a liberal education he would have been better able to read the times and change with them. Rome's enemies were farther away and campaigns could no longer be concluded in a season. A generation earlier Marius, in 107 BC reorganized the army by enlisting slaves and poor people, thus changing the character of the army from a citizen to professional army (Life of Marius, 9). The great military exploits of Lucullus were done during his long absences from Rome, during which time other men, not necessarily as good as Lucullus, but with the advantage of being in Rome where they could sway the crowd and argue in the senate, held office and with envious eye regarded Lucullus' Asian exploits as a threat to their own careers rather than a credit to Rome.

Lucullus, perhaps, just didn't understand the need to run a campaign of political rhetoric at home while campaigning against Rome's enemies abroad. The next generation of leaders, Pompey the Great, Julius Caesar, and finally, Octavian known as Augustus will demonstrate an ever increasing awareness of this vital blending of the military and the civic virtues.

LEADERS EMPHASIZING PRESTIGE AT THE EXPENSE OF DOMINANCE

Plutarch gives us several examples of politicians and men of learning who did not have it in them to politically dominate the historical scene they found themselves in. They had gained their prestige often through reputations for high moral character and political brilliance. They identified themselves and their principles with the highest good for Rome. They were reluctant, therefore, to bend with the times. Instead they saw flexibility as immoral compromise and made a virtue of inflexibility and intransigence in the face of the need for change and reform. Cato is a prime example of a man who identifies his own principles with the good of Rome. His inflexibility ultimately prevented him from actually helping Rome when Rome really needed his leadership. Instead he relied on his reputation as a highly principled man to build political coalitions. Eschewing a dominance strategy himself he sought to impose his will through Pompey and other military men. Cato liked to think he would not engage in bribery to influence the politics of his day. He nevertheless supported the most outrageous crimes of Pompey as long as they were done in the name of the republic.

Plutarch gives us a detailed look at the ways in which Cato cultivated his reputation and his prestige-oriented style of leadership. Plutarch tells us that even as a child Cato (95-46 BC) showed evidence of his resolute character. At age 14 Cato sets himself against the dictator Sylla. He also devotes himself to the study of philosophy and to the practice of justice, which he seeks to advance through rhetoric. (Life of Cato the Younger, 2-4)

Following the customary course he enters the Roman army. In the war to put down the slave revolt of Spartacus (73 BC), Cato, though given no opportunity to distinguish himself in arms, is commended for his conduct. Back in civilian life Cato excels at canvassing for votes and he begins to attract the envy of less accomplished politicians. (Life of Cato the Younger, 8)

Cato becomes renowned for his incorruptibility after rooting out corruption. In fact, he distinguishes himself as the sole true guardian of Rome's public treasury. Cato consistently places public service above private gain. He also punishes the many collaborators with Sylla in his criminal reign. (Life of Cato the Younger, 16-19)

In 63 BC a bankrupt nobleman, Lucius Sergius Catilina, conspired to destroy the Roman Republic, but the plot is found out by Cicero and the conspirators are tried and found guilty. Several important men in the city are potentially implicated and many urge clemency for the conspirators lest unrest spread. Cato alone holds out for the ultimate punishment for the Catiline conspirators. (Life of Cato the Younger, 22)

Cato fearing the rising power of Pompey and wishing to moderate Pompey's ambition allies with Lucullus against Pompey only to find that in so doing he is assisting Caesar in his more far-reaching ambition. (Life of Cato the Younger, 29-30)

By opposing Pompey's request for land for his veterans and Caesar's reasonable desire for honors such as enjoyed by others, Cato drives Pompey and Caesar into that partnership which, later, will overthrow the republic. Marcus Tullius Cicero begs Cato be more reasonable and save himself and the republic through small compromises rather than sacrifice both to abstract principle. But Cato continues to block Caesar's attempts at reforms. (Life of Cato the Younger, 31-33)

> Cicero, the orator, who urged upon him that it was perhaps not even right in itself, that a private man should oppose what the public had decreed; that the thing being already past altering, it were folly and madness to throw himself into danger, without the chance of doing his country any good; it would be the greatest of all evils, to embrace, as it were, the opportunity to abandon the commonwealth, for whose sake he did everything, and to let it fall into the hands of those who designed nothing but its ruin, as if he were glad to be saved from the trouble of defending it. "For," said he, "though Cato have no need of Rome, yet Rome has need of Cato, and so likewise have all his friends." –Life of Cato the Younger, 31

Seeing that the great men are intent on seizing power and that the people, far from fighting for the republic are happy to see the advance of a Caesar or Pompey if only they will bring some order to the city, Cato advises Cicero in Rome, Ptolemy in Cyprus, and the other Ptolemy in Egypt each to reconcile himself to the present situation and so save self and country. None follows his advice. As for himself, he refuses to even consider such a compromise with those who would alter the forms of the republic which had come down from ancient times. (Life of Cato the Younger, 35)

When, Pompey, Crassus, and Caesar form the first triumvirate in 60 BC they bribe the people to keep Cato out of office. (Life of Cato the Younger, 41-42) Pompey continues to assist in the rise of Caesar, not heeding Cato's warning that Caesar, once secure, would turn on Pompey. And Cato warns the people of the danger from such ambitious men.

> But Cato, before the voting began, went up into the place of speaking, and desiring to be heard, was with much difficulty allowed two hours to speak. Having spent that time in informing them and reasoning with them, and in foretelling to them much that was to come, he was not suffered to speak any longer; but as he was going on, a sergeant came and pulled him down; yet when he was down, he still continued speaking in a loud voice, and finding many to listen to him, and join in his indignation. Then the sergeant took him, and forced him out of the forum; but as soon as he got loose, he returned again to the place of speaking, crying out to the people to stand by him. –Life of Cato the Younger, 43

But the people do not stand by him and finally Cato, seeing that city in disorder and Pompey the least harmful of the contenders for sole rule, reconciles with Pompey. And with Caesar marching on Rome, Cato advises the senate to put all into the hands of Pompey. (Life of Cato the Younger, 48-52)

Unfortunately, by the time Cato relents and backs Pompey it is too late. Caesar has the army and the people on his side. As we know from Plutarch's lives of Pompey and of Caesar, Pompey is overthrown by Caesar at Pharsalia in 48 BC Cato follows Pompey to Egypt where Pompey is destroyed through the treachery of the Egyptians. Cato takes command and fortifies Utica. There he assembles his council of 300 Roman businessmen and some senators, urging them to stick together the better to stand against Caesar and, failing of that, the better to treat for peace with Caesar as a body rather than singly. The Romans in Utica have such confidence in Cato that they elect to follow him into combat against Caesar and resolve to free their slaves that these might join in the battle. Cato, rather than following through with freeing and arming the slaves immediately, while all are excited and ready to join him, equivocates and quibbles about the technical legality of such a commandeering of private property for the public defense and, so, loses the moment. (Life of Cato the Younger, 56-60)

> One of the assembly proposed the making a decree, to set the slaves at liberty; and most of the rest approved the motion. Cato said, that it ought not to be done, for it was neither just nor lawful; but if any of their masters would willingly set them free, those that were fit for service should be received. Many promised so to do; whose names he ordered to be enrolled, and then withdrew. –Life of Cato the Younger, 60

The senators undertake to do what is needed to fight for liberty but the merchants and money-lenders accept the dictatorship of Caesar. The cavalry arrives but cannot agree on the best plan for withstanding Caesar. During the fateful period of Cato's vacillation the businessmen resolve to oppose Cato and throw their lot in with Caesar. Cato leaves the businessmen free to embrace Caesarism and he evacuates the senators to safety. (Life of Cato the Younger, 61-64)

Seeing no way out, Cato chooses death over life under tyranny. He sups with friends and discusses philosophy and then passes his last evening reading Plato the philosopher. (Life of Cato the Younger, 66-68)

> When the company was broke up, he walked with his friends, as he used to do after supper, gave the necessary orders to the officers of the watch, and going into his chamber, he embraced his son and every one of his friends with more than usual warmth, which again renewed their suspicion of his design. Then laying himself down, he took into his hand Plato's dialogue concerning the soul –Life of Cato the Younger, 68

In the early morning hours, Cato takes his own life.

Plutarch's digressions on Cato's odd behavior which causes him to be ill spoken of reveal much about the flawed character of Cato.

> For he would often come to the court without his shoes, and sit upon the bench without any under garment, and in this attire would give judgment in capital causes, and upon persons of the highest rank. It is said, also, he used to drink wine after his morning meal, and then transact the business of his office; but this was wrongfully reported of him. –Life of Cato the Younger, 44

Likewise, Plutarch comments on Cato's unconventional views regarding marriage.

> Among many that loved and admired Cato, some were more remarkable and conspicuous than others. Of these was Quintus Hortensius, a man of high repute and approved virtue, who desired not only to live in friendship and familiarity with Cato, but also to unite his whole house and family with him by some sort or other of alliance in marriage. Therefore he set himself to persuade Cato, that his daughter Porcia, who was already married to Bibulus, and had borne him two children, might nevertheless be given to him, as a fair plot of land, to bear fruit also for him. "For," said he, "though this in the opinion of men may seem strange, yet in nature it is honest, and profitable for the public, that a woman in the prime of her youth should not lie useless, and lose the fruit of her womb, nor, on the other side, should burden and impoverish one man, by bringing him too many children. Also by this communication of families among worthy men, virtue would increase, and be diffused through their posterity; and the commonwealth would be united and cemented by their alliances." Yet if Bibulus would not part with his wife altogether, he would restore her as soon as she had brought him a child, whereby he might be united to both their families. Cato answered, that he loved Hortensius very well, and much approved of uniting their houses, but he thought it strange to speak of marrying his daughter, when she was already given to another. Then Hortensius, turning the discourse, did not hesitate to speak openly and ask for Cato's own wife, for she was young and fruitful, and he had already children enough. Neither can it be thought that Hortensius did this, as imagining Cato did not care for Marcia; for, it is said, she was then with child. Cato, perceiving his earnest desire, did not deny his request, but said that Philippus, the father of Marcia, ought also to be consulted. Philippus, therefore, being sent for, came; and finding they were well agreed, gave his daughter Marcia to Hortensius in the presence of Cato, who himself also assisted at the marriage. –Life of Cato the Younger, 25

Showing up at the senate half-dressed and half-loaded and treating his wife and daughter as brood-mares are queer behaviors in our, or Cato's, or any time. Such actions mark a man whose affections are seriously disordered through a lack of self-awareness about what is proper and improper conduct. Perhaps Plutarch includes these observations so we can make the connection between character, as manifest in personal conduct and success or failure of the leader. Just as he failed to properly order his personal and family life, so Cato failed to heed his own sound advice to others to accept some of the changes Caesar was introducing to the republic. The result was Cato's destruction at his own hand with Caesar's rise to power not seriously inhibited by Cato's protestations.

Another example of a prestige-oriented leader who did not know when to use the dominance strategy and force is Nicias the Athenian.

The Greek politician Nicias attempted to rely solely on the prestige option in his dealings with the Athenian people. Even when he was charged with a military command he refused to exercise the dominance strategy—thus bringing himself and the Athenian armies to ruin.

Dante places among the cowards who suffer in Hell, Pope Celestine V; his "great refusal" was his abdication in 1294, five months after his election, which allowed Benedetto Caetani to become Pope Boniface VIII, Dante's enemy.

Plutarch, who always sees good mingled with the bad in lives he narrates, would probably not place Nicias (c. 470-413 BC) in Hell, even if he believed in Dante's Hell, which, of course, as a pagan, he does not. And be sure of it, there is good in "poor reluctant Nikias, pushed by fate" as Robert Browning calls him (Balaustion's Adventure, A.D. 1871).

Nicias is a younger contemporary of Pericles who comes to prominence on the death of Pericles (Life of Nicias, 2). His virtue is mostly of a negative sort, consisting in avoidance of evil more than seeking the good.

> He observed that the people, in the case of men of eloquence, or of eminent parts, made use of their talents upon occasion, but were always jealous of their abilities, and held a watchful eye upon them, taking all opportunities to humble their pride and abate their reputation... Upon such considerations, Nicias declined all difficult and lengthy enterprises; if he took a command, he was for doing what was safe; and if, as thus was likely, he had for the most part success, he did not attribute it to any wisdom, conduct, or courage of his own, but, to avoid envy, he thanked fortune for all, and gave the glory to the divine powers. And the actions themselves bore testimony in his favor; the city met at that time with several considerable reverses, but he had not a hand in any of them. --Life of Nicias, 6

Now, managing the destructive envy of others is one of Plutarch's recurring themes. But Nicias does not so much manage the people's envy and redirect it to more healthful and productive emulation as he simply tries to avoid it. And while giving credit to the gods --and not being like Timotheus the son of Conon, the Athenian, who claimed his own merit was the sole cause of his victories, and assigning no credit to good fortune, until, at last, fortune deserted him, leaving him to failure (Life of Sylla, 6)-- Nicias refuses to take responsibility for his own talents. In public affairs Nicias acts as one afraid of the people; in warfare his successes are largely due to luck (Life of Nicias, 2).

The chief fault of Nicias --a grievous one-- is his unwillingness to use coercive legal and political means to stand up to the unprincipled men who, rising to power in the vacuum he allows, do so much harm to Athens. Instead he tries to rely solely on his own prestige to win over hearts and minds of the populace to opposing the impending war with Sicily.

> Besides all this, he did great mischief to the city by suffering the accession of so much reputation and power to Cleon, who now assumed such lofty airs, and allowed himself in such

intolerable audacity, as led to many unfortunate results, a sufficient part of which fell to his own share. Amongst other things, he destroyed all the decorum of public speaking; he was the first who ever broke out into exclamations, flung open his dress, smote his thigh, and ran up and down whilst he was speaking, things which soon after introduced amongst those who managed the affairs of State, such license and contempt of decency, as brought all into confusion. Already too Alcibiades was beginning to show his strength at Athens, a popular leader...Thus it fell out that after Nicias had got his hands clear of Cleon...he found everything carried away and plunged again into confusion by Alcibiades, through the wildness and vehemence of his ambition. --Life of Nicias, 8-9

In a State where there is a sense of virtue, a powerful man ought not to give way to the ill-affected, or expose the government to those that are incapable of it, nor suffer high trusts to be committed to those who want common honesty. Yet Nicias, by his connivance, raised Cleon, a fellow remarkable for nothing but his loud voice and brazen face, to the command of an army. --Comparison of Crassus with Nicias, 3

Failing to dissuade the people from the Sicilian expedition, Nicias, along with Alcibiades, is placed in charge of the venture. Here again we see in Plutarch's Lives that no one is wholly bad (or wholly good) for when called on to lead, even in a war he disapproves, he goes and does the best he can. So the Athenians sail to Sicily, 415 BC But as general, Nicias, eschewing once again a dominance strategy, fails to prosecute the war aggressively, even undermining, through his harping on the inadvisability of the expedition, the morale of his men (Life of Nicias, 14).

After some months of forbearing to attack, Nicias finds himself now the object of a planned Syracusan counter-attack. In the initial assault the Athenians vanquish the Syracusans. However, Nicias fails to complete the victory and the Syracusans regroup and return to fight again (Life of Nicias, 16). He besieges Syracuse in 141 BC and is so sure of victory that he little regards the approach of Gylippus with reinforcements from Sparta. But when Gylippus arrives fortune turns and the Athenians are beaten back (Life of Nicias, 17-19). Nicias is afraid to stay and equally afraid of the Athenian response at home if he retreats in defeat. Just as Nicias has finally decided on retreat and is about to quit his untenable position, a lunar eclipse frightens him off his plan. This delay will be extremely costly. The Athenians attempted retreat turns into a total rout, Nicias is captured; the Athenians killed or enslaved. Finally Nicias is put to death in 413 BC (Life of Nicias, 20-27).

So why did Nicias flounder so? Well, he is almost unique among Plutarch's Lives in being nowhere noted as having emulated any other great man of his age or of the past. Considering the great stock that Plutarch puts in emulation, this is surely not a coincidence. A better education (for Plutarch says nothing of Nicias' education) may have inculcated a greatness of soul that could have overcome his petty avoidance of evils and spurred him on to use his talents to the fullest. The limits on the spirit that has not been liberated by education is another Plutarchan theme, perhaps most explicit in his Life of Marius where he writes:

...if any could have persuaded Marius to pay his devotions to the Greek Muses and Graces, he had never brought his incomparable actions, both in war and peace, to so unworthy a conclusion, or wrecked himself, so to say, upon an old age of cruelty and vindictiveness, through passion, ill-timed ambition, and insatiable cupidity. --Life of Marius, 2

Ultimately, however, Nicias' turning away from responsibility --with such dire implications for Athens as she, denied the leadership of a just and wise man, turns to dangerous demagogues-- must be rooted in a willful refusal to employ the dominance strategy when it alone could do the trick. Nicias could not face the truth that his country needed him to assert control and direction. This willful ignorance persists through most of his public life. He will scold the people for going the wrong way, but he will not lead them another way, and so, in the end, the Athenians suffer the calamity that Nicias himself had predicted and Nicias dies tragically.

Pericles so embodies the prestige-oriented style of leadership that we can assign to the Periclean age the historical moment at which the prestige strategy came into its own as an alternative to the familiar dominance strategy. Nevertheless the praise of Pericles can sometimes hide the fact that the man had very real political faults. We believe that to some extent Pericles refused to wisely use the dominance option and so led his followers into a disastrous war. Instead of soberly assessing the risks of war with the Spartans he secretly manipulated his city into conflict with the Spartans and did not adequately prepare Athens for all out war. Pericles neglected development of the dominance strategy. Instead his historical accomplishment was to make the prestige strategy viable. In this great accomplishment however he neglected the dominance strategy to his and his follower's own peril.

> For heroes have the whole earth for their tomb; and in lands far from their own, where the column with its epitaph declares it, there is enshrined in every breast a record unwritten with no tablet to preserve it, except that of the heart. --The Funeral Oration Delivered by Pericles, from Thucydides, History of the Peloponnesian War, II, 34

Pericles (c. 495-429 BC) is so credited with the brilliance of Athens in the fifth century that the era is commonly called the "Periclean Age." His vision of Athens as a "City upon a Hill" ...for all .... The eyes of all people are upon us" and his opening of his fellow-citizens' eyes to see that same vision place Pericles as one of the most commanding, respected, and emulated statesmen of any era. But Pericles also comes down to us as a "model of mild and upright temper", with "capacity to bear the cross-grained humors of fellow-citizens and colleagues in office which made him both most useful and serviceable to the interests of his country" (Life of Pericles, 2).

He led the people through the power of his oratory, as taught by the most regarded tutors in Greece. He lead them prudently and toward noble goals because that education was also directed toward development of a worthy character and lofty purpose.

> But he that saw most of Pericles, and furnished him most especially with a weight and grandeur of sense, superior to all arts of popularity, and in general gave him his elevation and sublimity of purpose and of character, was Anaxagoras of Clazomenae...For this man, Pericles entertained an extraordinary esteem and admiration, and, filling himself with...elevation of purpose and dignity of language, raised far above the base and dishonest buffooneries of mob-eloquence. --Life of Pericles, 4-5

Pericles, the aristocrat, threw in his lot, politically, with the party of the commons (Life of Pericles, 7) and, thus, bridged the gap between the haves and have-nots which was a perennial source of discord in the Athenian commonwealth. While he rose to power by flattering the mob, once in power he refused the people in their passions and ruled for the good of all Athens, playing to people's hopes and fears.

> *...he turned those soft and flowery modulations to the austerity of aristocratical* and regal rule; and employing this uprightly and undeviatingly for the country's best interests, he was able generally to lead the people along, with their own wills and consents, by persuading and showing them what was to be done...he made them, whether they would or no, yield submission to what was for their advantage...he alone, as a great master, knowing how to handle and deal fitly with each one of them, and, in an especial manner, making that use of hopes and fears, as his two chief rudders, with the one to check the career of their confidence at any time, with the other to raise them up and cheer them when under any discouragement, plainly showed by this, that rhetoric, or the art of speaking, is, in Plato's language, the government of the souls of men, and that her chief business is to address the affections and passions, which are as it were the strings and keys to the soul. And yet, his urging the people to goodness would have been of little avail had he not such a reputation for goodness himself as to render his conduct the proof of his words.

> The source of this predominance was not barely his power of language, but, as Thucydides assures us, the reputation of his life, and the confidence felt in his character; his manifest freedom from every kind of corruption, and superiority to all considerations of money. --Life of Pericles, 15.

Pericles also understood that his person and reputation were coin to be spent wisely and that familiarity could breed contempt.

> He immediately entered, also, on quite a new course of life and management of his time. For he was never seen to walk in any street but that which led to the marketplace and the council-hall, and he avoided invitations of friends to supper, and all friendly visiting and intercourse whatever...For these friendly meetings are very quick to defeat any assumed superiority, and in intimate familiarity an exterior of gravity is hard to maintain...Pericles, however, to avoid any feeling of commonness, or any satiety on the part of the people, presented himself at intervals only, not speaking to every business, nor at all times coming into the assembly, but, as Critolaus says, reserving himself, like the Salaminian galley, for great occasions, while matters of lesser importance were dispatched by friends or other speakers under his direction. --Life of Pericles, 7

He used the treasury of the Greeks to rebuild Athens, saying to those who object that they have no cause to complain so long as Athens continued to protect Greece from her external enemies.

> That which gave most pleasure and ornament to the city of Athens, and the greatest admiration and even astonishment to all strangers...was his construction of the public and sacred buildings. Yet this was that of all his actions in the government which his enemies most looked askance upon and caviled at in the popular assemblies, crying out how that the commonwealth of Athens had lost its reputation and was ill-spoken of abroad for removing the common treasure of the Greeks from the isle of Delos into their own custody... --Life of Pericles, 12

The massive public works undertaken by Pericles employed many people and included reconstruction of the Acropolis under the supervision of the sculptor Phidias; the building of the Parthenon by Callicrates and Ictinus; and the building of the Propylaea or gateway to the Acropolis. (Life of Pericles, 13) These projects, completed over the period of the 440s and 430s BC left some of the greatest architecture ever produced and continue to stand, as Plutarch said, as "Greece's only evidence that the power she boasts of and her ancient wealth are no romance or idle story."

Make no little plans. They have no magic to strike man's blood and probably will themselves not be realized...might serve as a political slogan for Pericles. To those who complained of the cost of rebuilding Athens Pericles said, Okay, charge it to me, but I get the recognition instead of the city. They switched and bade him spend more public money. (Life of Pericles, 14)

Some today might say of Pericles' ornamentation of Athens that it was "merely cosmetic," meaning thereby that is was a beautification of the surface that did not change the essential structure or order of the city. The Greeks thought quite differently. The Greek word cosmos, often translated 'world', carries a root meaning of order and is the source of two English-language words you probably never associated together: cosmology, the science of the study of the order of the universe and cosmetology the art of beautifying the face and body which is an act of putting one's appearance in proper order. The role of the leader is to bring, out of chaos, order. By ordering his own affections (character) one can lead followers in the direction best for them, rather than in a self-serving manner or by merely appealing to their prejudices. By learning to order his speech (rhetoric) the leader acquires a tool needed to persuade followers. By balancing the legitimate concerns of all classes of society and by avoiding unnecessary and unjust wars the leader creates ordered society that reflects the order of the cosmos. And by promoting the arts and sciences the leader causes cosmic and civic order to be revealed through art, architecture and music.

Pericles' other achievement, restraining the peoples' passion for invading Sicily and confining Athens' ambitions to Greece, had force of law only for his lifetime, yet stands as a cautionary tale for every leader: a reminder that popularity and leadership are quite different things.

> The course of public affairs after his death [of the plague in 429 BC] produced a quick and speedy sense of the loss of Pericles. Those who, while he lived, resented his great authority...presently after his quitting the stage, making trial of other orators and demagogues, readily acknowledged that there never had been in nature such a disposition as his was, more moderate and reasonable...or more grave and impressive in the mildness which he used. And that invidious arbitrary power, to which formerly they gave the name of monarchy and tyranny, did then appear to have been the chief bulwark of public safety; so great a corruption and such a flood of mischief and vice followed, which he, by keeping weak and low, had withheld from notice, and had prevented from attaining incurable height through a licentious impunity. --Life of Pericles, 39

Indeed, Pericles' management of the early years of the Peloponnesian War was masterful. His maneuvering however appeared to be to steer the Athenian people into conflict with Sparta. He deliberately provoked the Spartans by insulting their allies and in myriad ways angering the Spartans. Pericles also seemed to endorse the intemperate approach of Alcibiades who was his ward.

We know the sad rest of the story. How demagogues, such as the brilliant and charming but utterly rudderless Alcibiades, flattered the people in their wildest fantasies of world domination and drove Athens onward to her downfall. By secretly encouraging Alcibiades while publicly counseling caution Pericles demoralized the city's leaders.

> When the war broke out, here also Pericles seems to have rightly gauged the power of his country. He outlived its commencement two years and six months, and the correctness of his previsions respecting it became better known by his death. He told them to wait quietly, to pay attention to their marine, to attempt no new conquests, and to expose the city to no hazards during the war, and doing this, promised them a favourable result. What they did was the very contrary, allowing private ambitions and private interests...to lead them into projects unjust both to themselves and to their allies--projects whose success would only conduce to the honour and advantage of private persons, and whose failure entailed certain disaster on the country in the war. --Thucydides, History of the Peloponnesian War, II, 65

As statesman, Pericles belongs to a small set of the greatest leaders of all time. For his contribution to the great art of the world, he stands alone.

> ...for the beauty and magnificence of temples and public edifices with which he adorned his country, it must be confessed, that all the ornaments and structures of Rome, to the time of the Caesars, had nothing to compare, either in greatness of design or of expense, with the luster of those which Pericles only erected at Athens. --Comparison of Fabius with Pericles, 3

Like all great leaders, however, he had his faults as well. Although he acted to restrain Athenians lust for war in his early years he incited lust for war as plans for the expedition to Sicily matured. In particular, he very much wanted and incited war against the Spartans. His disastrous plan to herd all Athenian subjects into and behind the city walls contributed to the outbreak of plague in Athens and ultimately to his own death. His wavering on the Sicilian expedition left Alcibiades in the driver's seat in terms of foreign policy. The ultimate cause for the destruction of Periclean Athens must be laid at the doorstep of the Peloponnesian wars and Pericles had welcomed indeed fought for that war policy.

Pericles is one of the first heads of state who attempted to combine the prestige and dominance strategies during his tenure in office. He, however, tended to avoid the use of force when it most mattered and thus he failed in his attempt. His judgment, therefore, was lacking in military matters. Instead of deferring to his generals he pushed for war when Athens was not ready for war. He used his prestige to further the war party. He knew that either Sparta or Athens had to rule—there was not room enough for two Greek powers as far as he as concerned. He had enough of a strategic vision to prepare for war but his sense of timing was poor to say the least. He must take his share of the blame for bringing plague and ruin to Athens, after he had raised it to glory only a few years before. He could not master the flexible use of both the prestige and the dominance strategies. Perhaps only Caesar ever managed to accomplish that feat for any period of time and that is why Caesar must be reckoned one of the greatest leaders of all time. To really appreciate Caesar's accomplishments we must first look at the men (Cicero, Pompey, et al.) who opposed him as these were truly worthy opponents.

Chapter 8

CICERO VERSUS POMPEY: AN ILLUSTRATION OF THE PRESTIGE AND THE DOMINANCE STYLES OF LEADERSHIP IN CONFLICT

We now wish to illustrate the impact of the prestige-oriented and the dominance – oriented leadership styles on the careers and lives of two men who exemplified these styles. Cicero emphasized prestige-related goals in his leadership style while Pompey emphasized the dominance style. Both men were in conflict with Caesar, who, unlike his opponents, could flexibly use both strategies. Obviously both Cicero and Pompey drew on both styles of leadership during their long and distinguished lives. Our point here is that each of these two men relied more exclusively on one style over the other and thus paid the price for neglecting one of the two poles of leadership. As in previous chapters we take Plutarch as our guide to these men's leadership styles.

WHO WAS CICERO?

Cicero was one of the greatest statesmen who ever lived. He is particularly important to us as the creator of a very distinct view of leadership—one which linked long-term success in leadership with morality rather than with 'expediency'. Because Cicero consistently argued that leadership (and success) followed from taking a consistent moral stance, he has been a problem for dishonest political leaders for 2000 years. Tyrants, in particular, have had to contend with the long-dead Cicero who haunts them from his books and from his grave.

Cicero believed that public service was integral to attainment of leadership virtues. If one could not affect events of one's own polity or community then one was not fully alive to leadership. In his own time, Cicero was fiercely dedicated to the Roman Republic, precisely because the republic provided ways in which ordinary citizens could influence the great affairs of state and thus could attain to leadership virtues. The politicians of his time, however, were not particularly interested in the glory associated with attaining to virtue. Instead, they were interested in mere power. Cicero traced the decline of the republic to the absence of real leadership among Rome's politicians. He hoped that the leaders of Rome, especially in the Senate, would chose to improve their characters and place commitments to individual virtue and social stability ahead of their desires for fame, wealth, and power. He often pointed to himself as an example of how to save the republic. It was, as if, he said "Observe that I place virtue and philosophy first and that this is the way we can save the republic." His increasingly frantic and bitter complaints that no one was following his advice was treated by Plutarch as a character flaw or a kind of vanity running throughout his public career. Modern historians too, have treated Cicero's increasingly desperate references to his own 'greatness' as an unbecoming petulancy in Cicero's character. But if we understand that he was trying to get his peers to imitate his behavior (on the ancient belief that imitation led to character and moral improvement), then we can be a little less condemning of his incessant references to his own accomplishments in his writings. In any case his accomplishments were considerable.

One can get a sense of how dangerous Cicero has been for tyrants down through the centuries by reading his *De Officiis* (On Duties; published 44 BC) alongside that of Machiavelli's *Il Principe* or 'The Leader" commonly known as 'The Prince'. *Il Principe* was published (in AD 1513) over 1500 years after Cicero's book appeared but was written as a kind of point by point rebuttal to Cicero's arguments in the *De Officiis*.

CICERO VS. MACHIAVELLI

Machiavelli used to say that he loved to imagine sitting down to dinner with great leaders of the past; to conjure up these great men until he could see them sitting across him at the dinner table with glass in hand; and to ask them to reveal their secrets of leadership to him. One wonders whether he ever imagined sitting down with Cicero. Surely he had and we can read the result of the conversation that transpired that night by opening the pages of Il Principe and then finding the passage in Cicero that inspired the outburst. Machiavelli apparently believed that in the realm of politics the dominance rather than the prestige strategy was far safer. It was after all far better to be feared than loved. Cicero, on the other hand, favored the prestige strategy:

> "The best of all means of looking after one's own interests is by winning affection… So here is a principle which has the widest possible application. a principle that ensures not only a man's safety but his prosperity and power: it is better to win affection than fear." - Cicero *De Officiis* p. 132.

While Cicero held that pursuing a moral course was most useful, most successful and most expedient, Machiavelli argued the exact opposite: the most expedient acts were often immoral acts. Machiavelli reminds us that prestige without dominance may often be both ineffective and immoral. Immoral because the leader could have chosen to enhance his/her strength and dominance but did not. That is why weak leaders, even when they are good men, may nevertheless be considered immoral. When their weaknesses lead to negative consequences for followers the leader must take responsibility for not making himself stronger.

On the other hand, leaders who rely solely on a dominance strategy underestimate the importance of prestige for achieving victories—particularly lasting victories. Machiavelli and many so-called leaders who lived after Machiavelli wrote, could not bring themselves to believe that a strategy of consistent honesty, integrity and morality was the best course a leader could pursue when considering the interests of his state. They could not hear the warnings of Cicero.

Cicero argued: *"The implication that something can be right without being expedient, or expedient without being right, is the most pernicious error that could possibly be introduced into human life."* Cicero *De Officiis*, p. 124 Whenever a political leader acted with justice and right, he served his followers well and improved the political culture of his state; and conversely whenever a leader acted without consulting justice and right, he inevitably led his followers and his state by a short route to chaos.

Although Cicero and Machiavelli disagreed on the fundamentals of leadership, we are sure Cicero would have agreed with Machiavelli when Machiavelli argued that there was nothing more difficult to take in hand, more perilous to conduct or more uncertain in its success than to take the lead in the introduction of a new political order.

Any leader must at some point attempt a new order of things, if only to take his followers in a profitable direction. Yet introducing a new order of things inevitably sparks fear, opposition and deadly hatreds. Cicero and Machiavelli both understood this-yet neither could see that a mixed strategy of prestige and dominance was the best course to take when introducing political change. Flexibility is key to good leadership.

DANGERS OF LEADERSHIP AS ENUMERATED BY CICERO

Taking on the responsibility of leadership always involves the introduction of a "new order of things" and is therefore quite perilous. Leadership should not be taken lightly because too much is at stake, both for the leader and the leader's followers. As Cicero constantly pointed out, leaders whether they like it or not exert profound moral effects on everyone around them. As discussed in the chapter on the science of emulation, we humans are wired, are pre-attuned, are 'set' to search for and then to imitate 'leaders'. Human beings involuntarily 'ape' salient qualities of others—and this faculty of imitation becomes fully engaged when exposed to a leader of power and eminence. This is partly what underlies the intense feelings of betrayal when a leader fails morally. To support his arguments that leaders were, whether they liked it or not, treated as *moral models*, Cicero pointed out that we tend to expect more from our leaders because we intuitively realize that they are the models we need in order to grow into integrity. If they fail us, our chances for that growth are diminished. Cicero was interested in the consequences of this failure both for the leader and for his followers. With respect to the leader, we vilify those leaders that fail us and are relentless in our persecutions and condemnations of leaders who turn out to be 'human, all too human'. Cicero unflinchingly pointed to the moral failings of leaders but never persecuted failed leaders (except perhaps for Catiline).

Cicero catalogued other threats to the leader. The leader not only is held up to inhuman moral standards by the public and his followers, the leader also must deal with the intrigues and envy of his closest associates as well. One might even consider it a law of history and of leadership that when a leader successfully achieves some amount of moral excellence he will immediately and intensely elicit two responses from his closest associates: 1) admiration bordering on awe and 2) envy growing rapidly into resentment and murderous hatred. Both responses are due to roughly the same psychic mechanism (see the chapter on the science of emulation, for a fuller discussion). When the imitation faculty is activated in a person eager to attain to eminence and leadership via exposure to a worthy model, the aspirant is confronted with two opposing motivational states: to continue to empathize with the model and thereby to attain a kind of psychic union with the model (this leads to the reaction of admiration and awe); or to block the empathy response. Blocking the empathy response throws the aspirant back on his own resources which are found wanting. The aspirant now both desires union and dreads it as some kind of challenge he cannot meet. This further exacerbates the aspirant's self-loathing. The model is then castigated and blamed for the sorry state the aspirant finds himself in. Yet every exposure to the worthy model is seen as a new condemnation of the petty response the aspirant followed when he refused empathy. The aspirant is then burned alive in the fires of his own resentment and envy of the model. Either the model must be destroyed or the aspirant must be destroyed.

In some ways we can see these aspirant/model dynamics at work in the relationships of several of the Plutarchan figures in this book. A very famous example, of course, is Brutus versus Julius Caesar. Indeed, one can take virtually any character who knew Caesar and discover their awe, admiration, fear and envy of Caesar. More on Caesar later.

Ultimately it is the responsibility of the follower/aspirant to leadership to move beyond envy and self-hatred into empathy with a worthy model. This is accomplished most easily when one uses 'God' as the model but we also need non-divine exemplars of leadership in order to grow into leadership. Until aspirants find ways to move beyond envy and resentment, the leader will be exposed to the hatreds, resentments, extravagant expectations and hopes of his followers. The Leaders' path is indeed perilous.

The next set of Ciceronian threats the leader is exposed to come from the leader's avowed enemies. Machiavelli saw these types of threats very clearly and counseled use of force, cruelty, guile, cunning and deception when dealing with enemies. A leader must possess *strategic cunning*—he must be able to use his wit and audacity to outmaneuver his enemies. All of the political skills displayed by Cicero are required when dealing with enemies. Yet even Cicero eventually lost the battle over his life with his enemies. Alexander, and thousands of years later, Lincoln (who read and re-read Plutarch throughout his life) counseled that the best way to eliminate your enemies was to make them your friends. The only way to do this, Cicero counseled, was to return good for evil whenever possible. We will return to this issue below but conclude that the prestige strategy (returning good for evil) does not work without some way to establish political dominance as well.

But we have not yet completed Cicero's catalog of threats the leader faces. Few can argue with the threats to the leader we have just detailed: those from his enemies (who are out to destroy him; from his followers (who will castigate the leader for even the slightest moral failings) and those from his closest associates (who will either admire the leader excessively or hate him excessively). But others may voice reservations when we claim that leaders face grave threats from the 'gods' or from spiritual realities that remain mysterious to science—yet operate with an awful certainty in human lives.

The Greco-Roman concept of hubris explicitly recognizes the clash between leaders and the gods. Cicero was profoundly aware of the danger of hubris for a leader or a state. When a leader displays unusual excellence of some kind, the gods begin to turn their gaze upon him. He feels a rise in temperature in the air around him but cannot attribute it to anything special so he carries on as if nothing special had happened. If he continues to grow in excellence and success, the gods then begin to discuss him and clash with each other over who will be his sponsor. The leader on earth, unaware of the attention he is getting from the gods will feel both a rise in temperature in the air around him and he will have an uneasy sense that he is being watched under any and all conditions.

As one or two gods begin to consistently favor him, situations that use to baffle him will seem easier and success will come easier as well. Now the crucial moment comes: will he attribute his successes to the gods (his sponsors) or to himself? If he attributes his successes to his own merit and excellences, the gods will become angry with him and then set him up for a fall. They will make life even easier for him than before and they will surround him with advisors who counsel recklessness –while calling reckless undertakings, instances of audacity. Soon the leader's successes go to his head and he exclaims, "What a great man am I!" Then the gods flay him alive on the coals of his next reckless adventure. Hubris is an outrageous form of arrogance and self-infatuation and thus successful leaders are most susceptible to its intoxicating dangers. When you begin to be noticed by the gods, it is time to learn humility as well as the difference between recklessness and audacity.

Cicero's life –especially as recounted by Plutarch, presents an extended lesson on how a leader can negotiate the perilous straits of leading in turbulent times, when much hangs in the balance including potentially one's own life. Like Cicero and Machiavelli, Plutarch understood that leadership was perilous. In his study of Cicero's life he gives us some clues as to how a leader can avoid the perilous pitfalls of leadership. The key, as always, was to strive for moral integrity. Cicero personified this striving after moral excellence—not in the sense of religious piety but rather in the sense of public spiritedness, service, duty, beneficence, goodness and trustworthiness. Let's look at Cicero's life to see how he pursued the strategy of prestige and thereby handled the burdens of leadership. He failed, however, in establishing his political dominance.

CICERO'S HANDLING OF THE BURDENS OF LEADERSHIP

The basic facts are easy to summarize: Born in 106 BC, six years before the birth of Julius Caesar, into a wealthy family, he desired and received a fine education, studying rhetoric and philosophy in Rome, Athens, and Rhodes. Like most ambitious young Roman men he made a name for himself as a lawyer in the Roman law courts. His eloquence and skill was such that he rose rapidly becoming quaestor in 76 BC, which made him a member of the Senate. In 63 he was elected consul, the height of the Roman political system. During his year as consul he put down the conspiracy of Catiline, for which he was awarded the title of "Father of his Country." Cicero, however, could not find a way to lead the Roman Senate into passing measures that would solve the primary problems of the republic: increasing social and economic inequities as the empire grew rapidly. The class conflict erupted into full political chaos, thus providing the means by which the strongman Caesar took power. Although Caesar restored order he did not relinquish political power, thus spelling the demise of Cicero's beloved republic. While Cicero looked for ways to restore the republic after Caesar was assassinated in 44 BC he attacked Mark Antony, in his public orations called the Philippics but his association with the young Octavian (later the Emperor Augustus) did not save him from Antony's revenge and he was killed in the wave of assassinations which began the triumvirate regime of Octavian, Antony, and Lepidus (43 BC).

Cicero lived during the waning years of the republic. Though he longed to save the republic from extinction he could not find a way to reconcile the warring factions that were destroying it. These were the traditional oligarchy of the Senate -- known as the optimates or 'best men of Rome' – and the self-appointed representative of the common people known as the populares. Most often the populares politicians were demagogues who had no understanding of the value of the rule of law or of political order. The oligarchic senators on the other hand displayed an exasperating reactionary and unyielding posture and seemed to have no understanding of justice and the grievances of the common man and so the common man was left to be preyed upon by the populares demagogues. Cicero was the only man capable of bridging the divide between these factions but finally was unable to do so.

Cicero could never find a comfortable home for himself in either political camp. To the optimates he was like the populares –dangerous 'new men' without respectable family histories and immoderate innovators etc; to the populares he was an intransigent reactionary. Cicero's perpetual oscillation throughout his political career, 'was he with the optimates or the populares?' exasperated his potential allies and made him vulnerable to enemies in both camps.

Cicero however managed to climb the ladder of the Roman political culture (quaestor, aedile, praetor, and consul) reaching the consulship in 63 BC It was during his consulship that one faction of the populares attempted a desperate gamble for power. The radical Catiline -- a restless young aristocrat in debt up to his ears and facing social and financial catastrophe for failure to pay those debts, had decided to stage a coup d'état. The assassination of Cicero was among his plans.

The young consul was therefore suddenly faced with a life or death crisis. He acted decisively. He used spies to intercept papers being passed between the conspirators and then published these papers to the Senate. The plot was exposed and the army quickly rounded up those involved. At this point Cicero uncharacteristically endorsed the death penalty for Catiline and his co-conspirators while Caesar recommended exile. The senate voted for execution and Cicero was hailed as savior and father of the republic.

Cicero's actions in crushing the Catiline conspiracy show that Cicero was capable of attaining to and exercising political dominance but like many other leaders before him he let the power go to his head when he called for the execution of the conspirators. This vengeful act damaged Cicero's prestige. Interestingly Caesar appeared to learn from the episode. He made it a point to extend clemency to his enemies no matter how dangerous –as long as they could henceforth be dominated politically.

Cicero's crushing of the Catiline conspiracy did not end the political discontent that fueled the crisis to begin with. No reforms addressed the needs of the explosive combination of desperate young aristocrats facing ruin and crowds of impoverished common men roaming the streets of Rome. Clodius, was another Catiline but with more political skills and protected to some extent by Caesar and Pompey and therefore infinitely more dangerous than Catiline. Clodius loathed and feared Cicero. He eventually waged a kind of crazy street war against him, hiring gangs to burn down his house on the Palatine Hill. Events were very quickly spiraling out of control—yet the Senate, even with Cicero's guidance, could not or would not enact reforms to address the legitimate grievances of Roman citizens in financial need. Thus these people were left to the unscrupulous 'leadership' tactics of the populares like Clodius and company.

Rome descended into chaos with the warring parties brawling like street gangs in the Forum and frequently burning down the Senate and houses of notables like Cicero and Cato. Clodius was eventually murdered himself in just such a street brawl. It is important to note that the violence on the streets of Rome simply represented the political deadlock at the center of Roman culture. Neither the aristocrats nor the populares could win the struggle over reform and thus Roman political and administrative activities were nearly brought to a complete halt thus negatively affecting the lives of the 100 million people under Roman rule at the time. Naturally, Rome's military enemies noted the chaos in the capital and began to make preparations for invasion. For both Cicero and Rome the situation was desperate but here Cicero's prestige-oriented leadership style failed.

Cicero could not seem to find the political means to broker a solution. Indeed no one in political life at the time could see any solution in sight. Both of the major factions saw no chance to win except through total annihilation of the enemy. Thus, the political deadlock at the center of the empire led to a desperately serious threat to Rome itself.

At this critical point in the story two options emerged for Rome. One represented by Pompey and the other by Caesar. We will see that Pompey offered a simple military dominance strategy for Rome while Caesar pursued both a prestige and dominance strategy.

ENTER CAESAR

At this most momentous juncture in the life of Rome Julius Caser returned from his triumphant military campaigns in Gaul. Caesar offered a series of political solutions for Rome but was unwilling to disband his armies, arguing cogently that he would then be at the mercy of Pompey—his enemy. Once again the conservatives in the Senate including Cicero bungled the opportunity of using Caesar intelligently. They obstinately refused to even negotiate with him. Caesar thus, decided to act, in order to both protect his own situation and that of Rome itself.

Cicero was then confronted with the stark truth that the very man who could quell the chaos and thus 'save Rome' would in the process destroy the legal structure of the democratic republic. His beloved republic would be destroyed—but Rome and the Roman people would be saved from violent self-destruction. Caesar would restore order by taking on dictatorial powers. The situation was impossible for Cicero.

Oddly enough, Caesar and Cicero basically liked one another. They were the two towering leaders and intellects of their time. They were without doubt 'world-historical personalities'. Their destinies were bound up with one another. Both were confronted with the same political –military crisis and both knew that only decisive action could save Rome. Yet Cicero would not fully ally himself with Caesar. Why not?

Plutarch makes much of the relationship between Caesar and Cicero in his analyses of the leadership style of Cicero. Caesar liked Cicero and admired his intellect. Cicero, in turn, remarked that Caesar's commentaries on the Gallic campaigns were of the highest literary merit—a verdict seconded by scholars down through the centuries. The two shared sumptuous dinners and really fine conversations. Yet there was a fundamental rift between the two of them with Cicero refusing to see the need for both a prestige and dominance strategy that Caesar represented. Caesar, on the other hand, thought they could work together.

Caesar tried ceaselessly to recruit Cicero to his cause, without success. Cicero later spoke bitterly of Caesar's destruction of the republic but it is hard to see how Caesar could have restored order without taking on some dictatorial powers. After all Cicero himself invoked dictatorial powers when putting down the Catiline conspiracy. The difference was that Cicero thought that Caesar would never relinquish dictatorial powers and that was what horrified Cicero.

Nevertheless, when Caesar was assassinated on the Ides of March in the year 44 BC, the conspirator Marcus Junius Brutus famously cried out Cicero's name as he proclaimed the reestablishment of the republic. But Cicero was horrified by the brutal act and quickly fled the scene. He probably realized that these murderers had not the talent to lead Rome.

FINAL BATTLES

Cassius and Brutus, the killers of Caesar, took the eastern half of the empire and faced off against Caesar's heirs: Antony, whom Cicero despised, and Caesar's 18-year-old adopted son, Octavian, whom Cicero both rather admired and fully distrusted.

Cicero thought he could control the young Octavian and so he revived his hopes for the republic. He reasoned that he could play Octavian against Antony and keep them from uniting until the armies of Brutus and Cassius were victorious. Cicero finally called down the gauntlet against Antony, writing 13 famous Philippics against him. These were stirring speeches to the Roman people calling them to fight Antony and to restore the republic. The Philippics were modeled on the Athenian orator Demosthenes' attacks on Philip the Great, whom Demosthenes portrayed as a tyrant. Antony was not amused.

Unfortunately for Cicero, Brutus and Cassius were defeated by Antony's armies at the Battle of Philippi in Greece and then Antony's henchmen came looking for him. Octavian deserted Cicero and formed a Second Triumvirate with Antony and a general of Caesar's named Lepidus. It immediately declared hundreds of senators to be public enemies and one of them was Cicero himself.

Fleeing from one of his country villas in a litter, Cicero was caught by the assassins in a wood and beheaded on the spot. Plutarch tells us he died in the brave Stoic manner sticking his head out from the litter so that his throat could be slit.

> "Cicero heard [his pursuers] coming and ordered his servants to set the litter down where they were. He...looked steadfastly at his murderers. He was all covered in dust; his hair was long and disordered, and his face was pinched and wasted with his anxieties - so that most of those who stood by covered their faces while Herennius was killing him. His throat was cut as he stretched his neck out from the litter... By Antony's orders Herennius cut off his head and his hands." --Life of Cicero, 36

It is perhaps with some irony that we read the story of Cicero's ending alongside the lesson Machiavelli derived from it. We mentioned above that Machiavelli believed that it was better to be feared than loved.

It is interesting that Machiavelli never understood that fear and love CAN exist together and indeed that the prestige (love) and dominance (fear) strategies MUST co-exist if we are to have order in human society. The two strategies were combined in Caesar's leadership style but Machiavelli did not see it. Cicero, on the other hand, could never mount an effective political dominance. Prestige was not enough. He chose the life of a philosopher who out of a sense of duty enters into the public fray in order to advance the welfare and dignity of his fellow citizens. He did not understand that public life required a commitment to a dominance strategy in addition to the prestige strategy. Instead he always believed that the prestige strategy was sufficient if the republic was preserved. That however was a big IF! Only political dominance could ensure the survival of the republic. The republic allowed men to act with real effect for the public good. It allowed for real service and real development of leadership. A public man with a vision and with eloquence could actually take the people somewhere! There was possibility and glory awaiting those leaders with an inspiring vision. For Cicero none of this kind of leadership was possible without public service.

Few leaders had developed more profound ideas on the ways in which public service could revolutionize the personality; order it, bring it to "a splendid integrity", allow it to step into leadership and find its moment of destiny. Only Edmund Burke comes to mind as someone who rivaled Cicero's accomplishments in the area of prestige-oriented political leadership. These two men led by argument and eloquence. They had no armies, only arguments and they put their faith in 'right reason' as the best hope for mankind.

The faith in 'right reason' in turn developed out of Cicero's philosophy of the role of 'natural law' in creating political order. He was the first individual to explicitly; clearly and unambiguously enunciate the basic idea of 'natural law theory.' It can be argued without exaggeration that natural law theory is the basic intellectual framework within which individual and political order has unfolded in the West over the last 2000 years. In his *De re publica* (On the Commonwealth, 54-51 BC) Cicero states:

> "There is a true law, right reason in accord with nature; it is of universal application, unchanging and everlasting...It is wrong to abrogate this law and it cannot be annulled...There is one law, eternal and unchangeable, binding at all times upon all peoples; and there will be, as it were one common master and ruler of men, God, who is the author of this law, its interpreter and sponsor." Book III, Chapter 22

Cicero's basic idea is that some transcendent force or personality (God) is the ultimate sovereign of any political order. No human being can claim ultimate sovereignty. Thus, there are clear lines of order and authority in the world that can be activated when we align ourselves with the natural law. This inherent order in the universe as expressed in our bodies and minds is brought to consciousness in the faculty of reason. The reasonableness of human consciousness and human Nature was a prime belief of Cicero's. He knew that it was tenuous and had to be cultivated and nurtured and fought for—but it was real.

What is more is that this transcendent God/authority was not an arbitrary force. Rather he manifests himself in 'right reason'. He chooses to manifest his beneficent and ordering presence through reason. He favors those conditions and choices optimal for human beings. Note that Cicero's formulation of the natural law favors development of radical individuality as it allows for freedom of conscience as long as conscience is informed by right reason. Thus the whole emphasis in the West on freedom of the individual and his conscience owes a great debt to Cicero. Cicero's formulation of natural law, furthermore, is an appeal to rational argument in settlement of disputes, to discussion, cooperation, and 'the Word' when working things out. Whenever any party wanted to settle disputes rationally Cicero's arguments were there telling them it was possible and preferable to war. How can any civilization ever repay a man for the gift of clarifying in one or two sentences the bedrock foundation of its moral order? But Cicero did just that for us and for his contemporaries. Unlike his murderers, he has therefore been held in affectionate regard by millions of grateful westerners ever since. Perhaps he was right when he said:

> "The best of all means of looking after one's own interests is by winning affection.... So here is a principle which has the widest possible application, a principle that ensures not only a man's safety but his prosperity and power: it is better to win affection than fear." - Cicero *De Officiis* p. 132.

There is no better summary of the prestige strategy than Cicero's.

We turn now to look briefly at that other (aside from Caesar) option available to the citizens of the Roman republic during their moment of crisis. That option was Pompey the Great (106-48 BC). We will see that in stark contrast to both Cicero and Caesar, Pompey embodied the dominance strategy in its purest form—though he never, like Sulla and other tyrants, abused the strategy. The dominance strategy is a strategy. It has intellectual content and does not consist of mere brute force. Real politique expresses the strategy well. No force is used unless absolutely necessary. Instead dominance is exerted through the rule of coercive law with financial pressure, police and military assets used as a back-up to the law or as a last resort.

Pompey was from a plebeian family and his father was ill-regarded by the people and the aristocratic factions. However, Pompey quickly overcame his origins by matching his noble character to his good looks. As was normal for a Roman youth, he entered military service and it is the dictator Sulla, pleased with Pompey's conduct of the wars, who honors him with the attribution "The Great." Pompey was honored with a triumph in Rome and as Sulla's power declined; that of Pompey's rose (Life of Pompey, 13-14).

During his early career Pompey was sent to Spain to put down Sertorius' rebellion. Pompey successfully pacified Spain. He also very wisely destroyed certain treasonous letters that fall into his hands that were penned by prominent politicians in Rome. He destroys them lest they become the occasion of continued civil war in the empire (Life of Pompey, 17-20).

> In the meantime Sertorius died, being treacherously murdered by some of his own party; and Perpenna, the chief among them, took the command, and attempted to carry on the same enterprises with Sertorius. Pompey therefore marched directly against, Perpenna. Pompey appeared suddenly with all his army and joining battle, gave him a total overthrow, Pompey guided by a high minded policy and a deliberate counsel for the security of his country. For Perpenna, having in his custody all Sertorius' papers, offered to produce several letters from the greatest men in Rome, who, desirous of a change and subversion of the government, had invited Sertorius into Italy. And Pompey, fearing that these might be the occasion of worse wars than those which were now ended, thought it advisable to put Perpenna to death, and burnt the letters without reading them. --Life of Pompey, 20

This is a prime example of how any leader who pursues the dominance strategy can and must use his intellect to pursue it effectively. Pompey's destruction of the treasonous letters saved both Rome and his own followers from years of useless bloodletting.

After the successful campaigns in Spain, Pompey returned to Italy to find the country convulsed by the slave rebellion of Spartacus. Pompey and Crassus ruthlessly put down the slave rebellion and share in the victory over Spartacus. Pompey then enjoyed a second triumph (Life of Pompey, 21).

While Rome wearied herself in civil war, pirates seized control of the seas. In 67 BC Pompey was sent out to suppress the pirates, under a proposal to grant him broad powers at sea and up to 50 miles inland. At this point he began to show some indications that he was aware that he needed to supplement the dominance strategy with a prestige strategy. He realizes that his rapid rise to prominence would create envy in others and therefore dangerous enemies. He begins a policy of consciously avoiding events that might elicit envy in his competitors.

Plutarch tell the story thus: '

> The assembly broke up for that day; and when the day was come, on which the bill was to pass by suffrage into a decree, Pompey went privately into the country; but hearing that it was passed and confirmed, he resumed again into the city by night, to avoid the envy that might be occasioned by the concourse of people that would meet and congratulate him. The next morning he came abroad and sacrificed to the gods, and having audience at an open assembly, so handled the matter that they enlarged his power, giving him many things besides what was already granted, and almost doubling the preparation appointed in the former decree'. --Life of Pompey, 26

Instead of relying solely on force in his war with the pirates, he shrewdly got some of the pirates to turn themselves in and betray their fellows, having received from Pompey an offer of mercy. In the space of three months Pompey ended the threat from piracy, such is the power of the combined dominance and prestige strategies (Life of Pompey, 24-28).

Pompey celebrated his third triumph having subdued to Rome, Africa, Europe, and Asia. Like Alexander before him, Pompey had essentially conquered the entire world before he was forty years old. However, just as he reached the heights, Pompey's figure turned tragic. Perhaps feeling that he no longer needed the prestige strategy he began to rely solely on his political dominance and ultimately his legions.

If he had to face ordinary opponents he undoubtedly could have just 'coasted' into lasting fame and retirement. But he faced some of the greatest leaders and political personalities of all time. These included Cato, Cicero, Crassus, and, of course, Caesar. Pompey, in short, underestimated his opponents. He appears to have done nothing while Rome burned in civil strife and while the republic was breathing its last. He let the Senate stymie any chance for reform and thus he let Rome descend into political chaos. Perhaps he was hoping that the Roman people would call for a new Dictator like Sulla to save them from the chaos engulfing them all. Whatever his reasons Pompey did nothing while Rome burned. He apparently believed that he had no formidable opponents. He apparently had forgotten about Caesar. In any case he underestimated Caesar.

> 'For Pompey, yielding to a feeling of exultation...and abandoning that prudent temper which had guided him hitherto to a safe use of all his good fortune and his successes, gave himself up to an extravagant confidence in his own, and contempt of Caesar's power; insomuch that he thought neither force of arms nor care necessary against him, but that he could pull him down much easier than he had set him up... --Life of Pompey, 57

And Pompey begins to listen to flatterers who lead him on:

> ...telling Pompey, that he was unacquainted with his own strength and reputation, if he made use of any other forces against Caesar than Caesar's own; for such was the soldiers' hatred to Caesar, and their love to Pompey so great, that they would all come over to him upon his first appearance. By these flatteries Pompey was so puffed up, and led on into such a careless security, that he could not choose but laugh at those who seemed to fear a war; and when some were saying, that if Caesar should march against the city, they could not see what forces there were to resist him, he replied with a smile, bidding them be in no concern, "for," said he, "whenever I stamp with my foot in any part of Italy, there will rise up forces enough in an instant, both horse and foot." --Life of Pompey, 57

And so the great struggle between Caesar and Pompey began. When Caesar crossed the Rubicon, all of Rome panicked. At this point Pompey could have used the prestige strategy to rally Rome into a united defense against Caesar. Instead, believing that his best chances lay with his legions outside of the city, he, the senate, and consuls fled the city. Pompey's blunder allowed Caesar to enter Rome peacefully. Caesar acted decisively to restore order to the city and allayed fears of a vengeful bloodbath. Thus, Caesar, within 60 days and with no bloodshed, restored order to Rome and became master of Italy.

Pompey then raised a great army in Greece and Asia with many of the best citizens allying themselves with him. But Pompey is overly cautious of engaging Caesar's army. He pursues Caesar, aiming to harass and wear him down rather than risking an assault. We may question whether Pompey is merely timid or is executing a cunning stratagem, but as long as he pursued this course Caesar was denied the outright victory that he needed to consolidate his power.

However, Pompey, fatefully, abandons his well-considered plan to follow the cries of flatterers and of the mob who urge him on to combat at Pharsalia in 48 BC Plutarch observes that it was not fated that Pompey should fight and lose to Caesar at Pharsalia. Pompey had more resources and could have delayed engaging until at a more favorable place, but he allowed himself to be swayed by faulty counsel.

> 'Heaven had not appointed the Pharsalian fields to be the stage and theater upon which they should contend for the empire of Rome, neither was he summoned thither by any herald upon challenge, with intimation that he must either undergo the combat, or surrender the prize to another. There were many other fields, thousands of cities, and even the whole earth placed at his command, by the advantage of his fleet, and his superiority at sea...Pompey, whose error had been occasioned by others, found those his accusers whose advice had misled him'. -- Comparison Pompey with Agesilaus, 4

After the defeat at Pharsalia, Pompey flees to Egypt where one of his own men basely kills him on the orders of the Egyptian king.

In sum we have three great men, Cicero, Caesar and Pompey. Cicero emphasized the prestige strategy and could not save Rome or himself. Pompey emphasized the dominance strategy and could not save Rome or himself. Caesar however combined the best of both the prestige and dominance strategies and thereby salvaged something valuable from the ashes of the republic..

Chapter 9

CAESAR: THE SYNTHESIS OF THE PRESTIGE AND DOMINANCE STYLES OF LEADERSHIP

INTRODUCTION

In previous chapters we have given nuts and bolts explanations and illustrations of key skills of leadership. In this chapter we take a step back and look at the development of the two major leadership styles as they interact over a single lifetime, in this case the lifetime of Julius Caesar. We are concerned now to get at the ways in which leadership skills synergistically support one another and how they unfold in the political and moral dilemmas of real life. We allow ourselves to address some of the philosophic principles that underlie classical conceptions of leadership character and of greatness. We find that it helps in everyday decision-making to have, at least an acquaintance with fundamental philosophical frameworks concerning what we now call 'leadership' as understood by the ancients. The ancients were concerned with problems of governance and political order. Although the yearnings for what Plato called the philosopher King were never realized (even in the life of a Marcus Aurelius) there nevertheless were a handful of leaders who deftly combined the best of both the prestige and the dominance forms of leadership in the ancient world. Their lives are instructive as they teach us that synthesizing the two styles, though difficult, is not impossible. One of these rare individuals was Julius Caesar.

Caesar is both the founder of the Roman Empire and the embalmer of the Roman Republic. The republic could not contain a man of his grasp, but out of the decay of the republic he initiated the imperial age of Rome's greatness.

According to Suetonius (The Twelve Caesars) Caius Julius Caesar lost his father at age 15. Plutarch's narrative, which is thought to have lost its opening chapter, lacks an account of the dictator's early boyhood, and opens with the teenager, the nephew of Marius the great rival of the tyrant Sylla, already attracting attention as a threat to Sylla. Early on Caesar showed the passion for distinction that marked his entire life. He remarked to friends that he would rather be the first man in an obscure village in Gaul than second man in grand and glorious Rome. And when, in Spain in his mid thirties, Caesar read a biography of Alexander the Great, he wept at the thought of how little he had accomplished compared to the Macedonian (Life of Caesar, 11-12).

Like Alexander, Caesar will be a conqueror and empire-builder. In battles, such as at Alesia where, outnumbered five to one, he simultaneously defeated two Gallic armies, one in the town, besieged by Caesar, the other behind him, besieging Caesar; he took as a trophy the Gallic king Vercingetorix; and finally subdued Gaul as a Roman province. Caesar proved a military leader worthy of his uncle Marius the great commander. But to his native talent for leadership and the organization he inherited from Marius, Caesar added what Marius lacked, a liberal education in philosophy and rhetoric. Thus equipped Caesar was ready to take his place as a leader of men not only on the battlefield but in the Roman forum and senate house.

> 'Sylla's power being now on the decline, Caesar's friends advised him to return to Rome, but he went to Rhodes, and entered himself in the school of Apollonius, Molon's son, a famous rhetorician, one who had the reputation of a worthy man, and had Cicero for one of his scholars. Caesar is said to have been admirably fitted by nature to make a great statesman and orator, and to have taken such pains to improve his genius this way, that without dispute he might challenge the second place'. --Life of Caesar, 3

As public speaker and writer of persuasive prose, Caesar was second only to Cicero among the men of his generation. But Cicero was no military leader, just as Marius was no deep thinker or civic leader. In Caesar, military command and political strategy combine. His victories on the field were followed by election to high office not merely chronologically, but as Caesar had planned, as an integration of the martial and civic virtues in one complete man. Indeed, we know in detail of Caesar's victory at Alesia, and his other victories in Gaul, from Caesar's own Commentaries. And even while campaigning, Caesar constantly was sending dispatches back to Rome in, perhaps, the first ever military public relations campaign.

As, under Caesar, the government of Rome began to resolve first on a few and finally one man, the place for orators and political theorists such as Cicero grew smaller. Indeed, as the Republic collapsed, Cicero spent much of his public career lending his talents to one or another of the various strong men who sought legitimacy through Cicero's skillful use of rhetoric. Caesar, having mastered that art himself, passed over Cicero and, for his first triumvirate enlisted Pompey and Crassus. This trio of Caesar, Pompey, and Crassus ruled Rome for from 60 to 54 BC Caesar's choice of co-rulers demonstrated his foresight and resourcefulness.

Pompey, known as the Great because of his early military and policing successes, was, as an ally, less of a threat to Caesar than he would be as an open rival, at least in the early rise of Caesar. But Caesar would be first, not one of three. And Caesar saw, from the beginning that a grand struggle between these two for domination of Rome was inevitable. Therefore he planned for the conflict while Pompey did not. Caesar's bonuses to his soldiers and promises of lands for them to retire to after the wars cemented them to him. His mild and lenient treatment, even of opponents whose lives he spared, and the reasonableness of his request for nothing more than the honors conferred on Pompey, were shrewd propaganda. After the death of Crassus, as the struggle between Pompey and Caesar escalated, Pompey was advanced to sole ruler of Rome, while Caesar was outlawed. But when Caesar marched on Rome the unprepared and uncomprehending Pompey fled with most of the senate. Caesar, officially enemy of Rome, illegally brought his armies into the city and then pursued, engaged, and defeated the legally constituted government-in-exile and came off as the savior, not enemy, of Rome. In a moving scene at the beginning of the 1960s Hollywood motion picture Cleopatra,

Caesar surveys the many Roman dead slain at the battle at Pharsalia in 48 BC, and declares, convincingly, "'Twas Pompey wanted it so; not I."

And so history remembers it for in this case the victor literally wrote the history.

The third triumvir, Crassus, was never a political rival for Caesar. The low nasty money-grubbing character of Crassus alienated him from the people's affection and from any serious chance at a successful public course of honor. And his military judgment was faulty. In fact, later, after serving Caesar's purpose as sometime ally, Crassus, goaded on by the wily Caesar, set forth on a disastrous expedition to Parthia where he and a huge Roman force were annihilated in 53 BC What Caesar saw in Crassus was money. Not money to enrich himself, as Crassus had done, but money for what it could do. Caesar observed, as others had not, that in the corruption of the late Republic, the traditional course to leadership --military success recognized in a triumph followed by stump speeches calculated to get the conquering hero elected to a consulship, had to be augmented with bribes for votes. It was Crassus' money that Caesar used to buy those votes. He also went deeply into debt buying today's honors with tomorrow's money.

> 'He was so profuse in his expenses, that before he had any public employment, he was in debt thirteen hundred talents, and many thought that by incurring such expense to be popular, he changed a solid good for what would prove but short and uncertain return; but in truth he was purchasing what was of the greatest value at an inconsiderable rate'. --Life of Caesar, 5

Early in this life, Plutarch presents Caesar's advantageous use of money. After bribing his way to freedom from Sylla's henchmen, the boy Caesar flees Sylla only to be captured by pirates. Again, in a pattern that will recur in Caesar's life, he uses money to good advantage. When the pirates demand 20 talents ransom he jokes that they must not know who he is, else they would have asked for more. Ransomed, released, and then returned with reinforcements, he makes good on another boast, one the pirates also mistook for a joke, that he would see them all crucified (Life of Caesar, 1-2).

In the episode with the pirates, Caesar gives early evidence that, as Plutarch writes:

> 'Caesar was born to do great things, and had a passion after honor, and the many noble exploits he had done did not now serve as an inducement to him to sit still and reap the fruit of his past labors, but were incentives and encouragments to go on, and raised in him ideas of still greater actions, and a desire of new glory, as if the present were all spent'. --Life of Caesar, 58

It was a passion unlimited by fear of death, of which Caesar famously said that it was "better to suffer death once, than always to live in fear of it."

Death came to Caesar, as we all know, at the hands of assassins on the Ides of March, 44 BC The first blow was struck by Vile Casca; the final blow by Marcus Brutus who was as a son to Caesar and whose life Caesar had spared after the battle of Pharsalia. The death of Caesar did not restore the ancient Republic. Nor, indeed, did the conspirators evidence any forethought for the organization of Rome and her empire after dispatching Caesar. Caesar's blood proved the seed of bloody civil war and Rome knew no internal peace until another Caesar, Octavian Augustus, restored order and ended all hopes for revival of the traditional liberty of Roman citizens to govern themselves through freely elected officers. But thanks to the bold vision of Julius Caesar, Roman order spread to Gaul and Britain and created the Western World.

EVALUATION OF THE CHARACTER OF CAESAR

Caesar was a man of wide learning and culture who excelled at everything he undertook. He was possessed of extraordinary personal charm, and regularly elicited the most intense personal reactions in the people around him, who included some of the greatest men and women who ever lived. Even his personal relationships with women were extraordinary. When his first wife, to whom he was quite devoted, unexpectedly died, he re-married and proceeded to engage in a series of highly publicized extra-marital affairs that fed the political legends gathering about him as his fame grew. His long affair with Servilia, the step-sister of Caesar's rival Cato, and mother to Brutus the assassin and, of course, the affair with Cleopatra, Queen of Egypt, whose exceptional beauty, learning, ambition and political shrewdness first confounded and later complemented Caesar's talents were legendary even in Caesar's own lifetime.

Caesar's struggles, friendships, and loves among men and women illustrate that striking fact about Caesar's character and life: His friends, enemies and lovers were some of the greatest personalities of all time. Thus, amongst his enemies in the political realm, we find Cato and Cicero, universally considered among the finest political thinkers and tacticians of all time. On the battlefield Vercingetorix the Gaul and Pompey, Caesar's rival and Roman general, were two of the finest military minds in history. Finally, there were the women-- those he loved and those he used, and sometimes both loved and used--who were extraordinarily talented both politically and intellectually. The cast of characters in Caesar's life illustrates Plutarch's central claim that those who would be great leaders must choose to surround themselves with great leaders. In other words to be a leader you must choose to *emulate* those who challenge and inspire you.

The models Caesar chose to emulate, both among friend and foe, were the greatest men and women of the age. Cato (called "the younger" or "the philosopher") stands out as Caesar's nemesis. All through Caesar's rise to power, there was Cato, trying to hinder him. This prompts a question about leadership and the relation of the leader to others, a question that comes up again and again in Plutarch's Lives and in the biographies of other great leaders. Did Caesar learn his leadership skills from his adversaries like Cato–or vice versa? Did a Caesar call forth a personality like Cato's to oppose him? Very likely there is a synergy of Caesar's actions challenging Cato who then was forced to rise to the occasion or be defeated. When Cato did in fact respond to Caesar's challenge, Caesar was forced to learn new skills and to grow or be defeated by Cato and his conservative allies. One can learn as much about leadership from one's adversaries as from one's friends or mentors.

Caesar's mind was unusually sharp and strategic, even compared to the extraordinary men who surrounded, supported, and opposed him in the waning days of the republic: men like Cato, Cicero the orator, and Crassus and Pompey, the military commanders. In the end Caesar outwitted them all.

A great orator and politician, he could also think well and write well. More astonishing still was that he wrote his masterpieces while conducting incessant warfare against the Gallic tribes of the North. Modern complaints of the hardships of a writer's life pale into insignificance when compared with what Caesar had to face when he was producing his masterworks. He wrote while under live attack and imminent annihilation at the hands of the hordes of Gallic warriors. Caesar in his commentaries on these battles, eschews the mealy-mouthed outpourings of artistic angst such as we get from most of the writers infected with the sentimental bilge of this modern 'psychologic' age. Instead he gives us matter-of-fact accounts of how Caesar systematically defeated one tribe after another and then imposed his and the Roman will on all of Gaul. Reading Caesar's commentaries drives home the fundamental lesson that leadership is finally about *domination*; the imposition of one's will on another.

In Caesar's case domination involved the synthesis of both military and rhetorical excellence. The style of the commentaries--straightforward, stately, and crisp--reveal a brilliance of Mind that animated every scene in the commentaries. Indeed Caesar rivaled Cicero when it came to written and spoken rhetorical eloquence. His commentaries on the Gallic wars are literary masterpieces as well as brilliant displays of rhetorical argument in support of his military and political goals.

Without a doubt he was a military genius. Furthermore, unlike Pompey, he knew how to use political discretion when it was required to consolidate his military gains. He was bold and fearless, displaying amazing physical courage in battle, lightning speed when pursuing the enemy and amazing strategic cunning when defeating enemies who often had larger and better-equipped armies than did he. Finally, he was an effective administrator and knew how to govern well. After he had pacified Gaul and set up its administration it remained a stable Roman province for centuries thereafter. In the few months in which he was given virtually unfettered powers to rule in Rome, he brought political order to Rome and its empire, reformed and rationalized the calendar, passed poor relief laws (thus mitigating violent expressions of class conflict) and rationalized the international tax system that supported both Rome and the provinces. The Emperor Augustus later used Caesar's original plans to administer the empire and they worked quite well for centuries despite repeated catastrophes of invasions, epidemics, religious fanaticism, economic upheavals and mediocre and barbaric emperors.

THE CONCEPT OF THE 'MOMENT OF DESTINY'

Interestingly, while Plutarch mentions a variety of episodes from Caesar's life to illustrate his multifaceted character, he chooses to emphasize just one such episode as crucial for his leadership development: the 'crossing of the Rubicon'. This was Caesar's 'moment of destiny'. Given the greatness of Caesar's character it turned out also to be a moment of destiny for the world.

The Romans had an almost mystical sense of how this 'moment of destiny' appeared in the life of the person called to leadership and how it elicited greatness when the individual opted to go with his destiny.

Cicero, the subject of another of Plutarch's Lives has left volumes of his speeches, letters to friends, and philosophical treatises. In his 'Dream of Scipio', Cicero has Scipio Africanus, destroyer of Hannibal and conqueror of Carthage, appear in a dream, to his adopted grandson the young Scipio. The elder Scipio Africanus reveals to the younger Scipio fundamental truths of life, most importantly the pursuit of the virtuous life, which in turn required confrontation with one's 'moment of destiny'. He says to the young Scipio:

> "...It will be your duty to devote to your people the full, splendid, benefit of all your integrity, talent and wisdom." ...When you attempt so to do..."two divergent paths of destiny will open up before you. For when your life has completed seven times eight circuitous revolutions of the sun, and when these two numbers, each of which is regarded as possessing some quality of perfection, have in their natural course brought you to your supreme moment of destiny, that is the time when the whole Roman state will turn to you and all that you stand for, the Senate, every right-minded citizen, our subject allies, the entire Latin people. The fate of the whole country, at that juncture will depend on you and you alone"

For Cicero and for most of the other great men of Rome the 'moment of destiny' involved a crisis and then a decision or choice between two divergent paths of action. It was understood that when a choice was made it would have momentous consequences for both the individual and for the public good.

Classical authors like Cicero and Plutarch believed that a person's destiny was bound up with the moral choices they made each day. They believed that all of the little choices we make result in formation of a consistent "character" and that, at last, it is this character that yields greatness and leadership when confronted with a crisis and moment of destiny. Moral splendor in the ancient sense, then, should not be confused with modern degradations of the term.

Morality --more than simply doing good and avoiding evil-- was and should be considered as a revelation of nobility of spirit. As the human individual is unique and unrepeatable, so moral splendor and nobility of character are infinitely varied and unpredictable. Only a moment of destiny can elicit the revelation of a person's true character. The decision taken in a moment of destiny is fraught with consequences both for the individual himself and for the State.

Plutarch argues in his "Lives" and shows us in his Life of Caesar that there is no better way to become a great Leader than to be confronted with a moment of destiny, when, through habits of character-building one has prepared for it. Often bringing with it some anguish, the Moment of Destiny is always a crisis and a gift of the gods. When the Moment comes all that you have to fall back on is your character. And if that character, forged in the crucible of thousands of daily and seemingly trivial choices, is lacking, you will likely not be able to find the nobility in your spirit and come through the crisis enriched rather than destroyed.

We will describe Caesar's 'moment of destiny' later in the chapter. Suffice it to note here that while other writers have seen the episode as decisive in some way for Caesar and for the history of the world, Plutarch alone shows us what precipitated the crisis and what character traits of Caesar's were constellated by the crisis and therefore what moral forces determined the outcome for both Caesar and the World. For Plutarch the character trait most determinant at this most precipitous point in the history of the World, where so much hung in the balance, was *audacity*—Caesar's sheer, caustic, intransigent and marvelous audacity!

Audacity is an unyielding and almost reckless belief in one's own star. But to be sustained against time and trial that belief in turn requires a whole set of background beliefs that include the following: individuals 'count'; they matter; they are of ultimate significance. Therefore the 'thing' of ultimate value in the universe is the unrepeatable, unique event we call 'character' or 'individuality'. This in turn implies that the 'thing' of greatest and ultimate value is unpredictable and cannot be controlled or reproduced at will. All that we can do is reverence it and try to predispose ourselves to its influence.

Individuals, furthermore, are given a destiny by God, the 'Universe', the 'stars' or the 'nature of things'. This divine will, furthermore, recklessly puts the fate of the world into the hands of these individuals. This handing over, by God, of power to the individual tells us something about God: God must be madly in love with the individual to put so much power for good and ill into his or her hands. It seems to us mortals a reckless act. God gambles that his beloved mortals will make the 'right' moral decisions when confronted with a moment of destiny that holds consequences for both the individual and the public good. God favors those few who exhibit the audacity to love, and to act, on their own fates. In a sense then, the man who recklessly gambles all on his 'star', or his fate, is emulating God himself in certain respects, as God seems to gamble all on the individual human being making moral decisions in a situation of crisis. God loves the individual who is willing to trust in his destiny and star by drawing on the audacity and fearlessness of his immortal spirit. What a gamble for both man and God! Who is more audacious here: God or man?

These, as we read Plutarch and the other classical authors, are some of the background metaphysical and religious assumptions involved in the great concept of the 'moment of destiny'. Though dramatic and somewhat obscure, they ring true to us and may help us when our individual moments of destiny arrive inviting us to leadership and responsibility.

EARLY LIFE

We will come to the episode wherein Caesar, in his moment of destiny, audaciously gambles on his star and crosses the Rubicon. To fully understand that episode however we will need to fill in some of the background on Caesar's life, pointing out wherever we can the evidence that Caesar is learning or acquiring leadership skills that will eventually support him when he faces his moment of destiny.

Two things stand out in the early life of a person destined for leadership: ambition and authority. The young Caesar had both qualities in abundance. *Ambition* is an energy that fuels the drive for eminence. Authority is aura or ruling power one exerts over followers.

You've got to want to shine, at least occasionally if you are going to acquire *authority* to rule. Ambition also gets you through years of emotional exile before you have found your footing, while you are facing and overcoming obstacle after obstacle, from petty humiliations to tempting sideshows, while your enemies seek to derail you and your own fears seek to undermine you.

Authority, on the other hand, can be defined as that set of attributions people assign to a leader that allow these people to accept guidance from the leader. Authority, in other words, is given to a leader by people looking for guidance. It is dependent, however, on the leader acting to consistently deliver good advice. Thus, the primary reason why people look to a given individual for guidance is that that individual has given good advice in the past. Ultimately, then authority comes from the abilities of the leader as reflected in consistent and high quality 'performances' in the past. This is a round about way of saying that fundamental to leadership and success is thorough preparation: i.e. to know your stuff. When you have gained a reputation for knowing your stuff, people will then treat you as an authority. If you have also developed a moral compass to guide your life it can be said that you now are ready to achieve 'prestige'.

People will also treat you as an authority, at least for a short while, if you hold some credentials or some office. If you have earned a Ph.D. or M.B.A. for example, of if you have been elected to public office, you are often given the benefit of the doubt until you prove otherwise. Now, if you are someone like Caesar, who both 'knows his stuff' and has been elected to public office then you will possess authority and people will, to some extent, act deferentially toward you. As is commonly understood, authority, whether derived from know-how, office or both can be used for both good and ill ends. The important thing for leaders, however, is that authority is necessary for effective leadership as it allows the leader to rapidly recruit followers and to steer them in the right direction.

The young Caesar certainly displayed huge reserves of authority, ambition and early forms of audacity. Although he was born into one of the oldest patrician families in Rome, the Julii, he had no immediate sponsor or protector who could guide his rise to the top. This lack of a sponsor was due largely to the fact that his family was tarnished by its association with Marius, the enemy of Sulla—then Dictator of Rome.

Despite his vulnerability, the young Caesar openly and publicly defied the murderous tyrant Sulla who had demanded that all relatives of Marius either be put to death or made politically unviable via divorce or some other form of ostracism. In 82 BC, when Caesar refused to obey Sulla's order to divorce Cornelia (a Marian relative), he was ordered to appear before Sulla. Now Sulla was known to arbitrarily order the execution of an interviewee who had opposed his demands in any way and Caesar did so in an almost brazen manner. Caesar was all of 20-21 years old at the time of the interview. One can only imagine what the young Caesar must have felt while standing or kneeling in front of this tyrant who had murdered his relatives and was now threatening him. No reliable accounts of the interview have survived but we do know that instead of acceding to Sulla's demands, Caesar did not divorce his wife but left Rome and did not return until Sulla's death two years later.

While abroad he performed minor services for the State and while engaged in these tasks he was captured by Pirates who demanded a huge ransom for the young noble. Neighboring subject allies of Rome raised the funds and ransomed him. During his captivity however, Caesar had the audacity to tell his captors to their faces that he was going to have them all crucified! His captors smiled at the impudence of the young lord and carried on with their drinking. That he escaped with his life was remarkable in itself but that he, in fact, kept his word and returned a few weeks after his release to hunt down the pirates and have them crucified was more remarkable still. Caesar had no official sanction or authority to execute this judgment on his captors. It was quite a risky act for the young Lord to take, as the pirates were quite likely operating under the protection of local and powerful potentates. Nevertheless, Caesar carried out his vengeance regardless of the dangers involved. This episode signaled to all who might care to notice that Caesar was not a man to be spuriously threatened or trifled with. His actions also certainly displayed that uncomfortable combination of boldness, bravery and near recklessness that we call audaciousness.

Upon returning to Rome Caesar quickly got himself involved in politics by attempting to prosecute (for corruption) certain provincial officials (former allies of Sulla). He lost the prosecutions but gained a reputation for oratory and began to acquire the leadership skills of the 'right use of public speech' or *rhetoric* and '*political discretion*'.

He very shrewdly began to ally himself with the *populares*, the politicians who opposed the conservative clique of Senators. The conservatives intransigently blocked even the mildest of reforms aimed at mitigating the plight of the common man and the burdens on the provinces. The struggle between the conservatives and the *populares* soon bogged down into political grid-lock, with the republic's important issues going unresolved. Denied political redress of their grievances, the *populares* eventually entertained overthrow of the republic. Caesar cunningly skirted association with these extra-legal maneuvering or radical measures, at least for the time. While his open sympathy for the just claims of the *populares* gave him a following among citizens who felt left out of the governance of their state, his careful avoidance of too close a connection with the radicals spared him from banishment or severer punishments handed out to other politicians who dared to stand with the radicals. We will see later that he used his developing rhetorical skills to mobilize and educate these followers when he wrote his commentaries on the Gallic wars he was prosecuting in Gaul…but more of this later.

The most important political figure in Rome at that time was Pompey whose spectacular military victories in the east commanded the loyalty of the armies. Pompey, however, vacillated between the *populares* and attempts to curry favor with the conservatives. Caesar's political policy slowly began to focus on the task of preventing Pompey from going over to the conservatives and instead to enter into an alliance with himself and with Crassus, then the richest man in Rome. This First Triumvirate (literally "three men") of Caesar, Crassus and Pompey became Caesar's vehicle to oppose the conservative Senate.

These deft political maneuvers signaled Caesar's mastery of the leadership skill of political discretion. This skill involves the ability to form strategic alliances with individuals and groups who share your interests. It involves a bargain -- you help me here; I help you there. Success depends on delivering your share of the bargain, at least enough to compel the others to deliver on their share. Caesar certainly made it a point to deliver the goods to his fellow potential triumvirs. Doing so was the only way he could lure Pompey and Crassus into such an alliance.

In 69 BC, Caesar helped Pompey to obtain the supreme command for a new war in the East—a favor Pompey would not forget. Rome had its eye set on seizing the riches of Syria and Pompey would be just the man to do so. Ridding Rome of Pompey also allowed Caesar to take over leadership of the *populares*. In Pompey's absence Caesar became the head of the popular party. When his first wife died he took the unusual step of giving her a public funeral oration and a fine burial. This act of public devotion made him even more popular with the plebs. We will never know if Caesar truly was devoted to this his first wife. Given the earlier refusal to divorce her despite the threat of death or banishment, our own feeling is that he was.

In 63 BC he was elected *pontifex maximus* (high priest), allegedly using Crassus' money to buy votes. Later that year Catiline, an impoverished noble who was so far in debt that he was in danger of losing all combined with other young men in similar financial straits and devised a plan to throw Rome into political chaos, take control of government, and enrich themselves at the public trough. Cicero, Consul (or chief magistrate) at the time, very deftly uncovered the plot and uncharacteristically advocated that the conspirators be executed. Cato the Younger also called for execution as he saw the conspirators as enemies of the Senate and the People of Rome. Caesar, however, advocated banishment rather than death for the conspirators. This enraged Cato, and when, during the debate Caesar received a slip of paper, Cato believing that the message was from pro-Catiline forces demanded that Caesar read the message aloud, right then and there in the senate. Caesar, of course, demurred, claiming it was a private message with no bearing on public affairs. Cato, however, persisted, and then finally Caesar relented and began to read the message. It turned out to be a love note from Cato's sister Servilia to Caesar! While all of the other Senators had a fine laugh over the matter Cato developed an almost fanatical and abiding hatred of Caesar.

After his first wife died, Caesar began to treat marriage as Sulla and the rest of the Roman political establishment did --as a political matter, a way of creating or cementing political alliances. Now, it was commonly known that Caesar was carrying on an affair with Servilia, but when Caesar's second wife, Pompeia, was accused of having an affair with a disreputable young nobleman Clodius, Caesar quickly obtained a divorce, saying, "Caesar's wife (i.e. the wife of the High Priest) must be above suspicion." Some historians claim that Caesar manufactured these suspicions against his wife so that he could divorce her and re-marry in such a way as to further his political ambitions. He later did just that.

In 59 BC he married Calpurnia- -whose father Piso was a docile politician whom Caesar could depend on to look after his interests when Caesar himself no longer held the Consulship. In the same year, his alliance with Pompey and Crassus began to yield fruit. Pompey returning from the Asian campaigns came back with immense booty, filling the coffers of the Roman State. He had conquered huge and wealthy provinces like Syria and Anatolia. He had also wiped out the problem of piracy in the Mediterranean. In short he had performed immense services for Rome and thus was wildly popular.

Cato and other conservative senators feared Pompey would use his popularity to set himself up as dictator, destroy traditional liberties of Roman citizens, and make the Senate powerless. The senate's short-sighted blocking of Pompey's requests for money or lands as just rewards for his soldiers practically forced Pompey into the arms of Caesar and Crassus. Caesar's strategy of an alliance with Pompey, the only living Roman general who could rival Caesar and with Crassus, the one man in Rome with the money to pay for the grand enterprise, had now matured.

With this marriage of money and military might to support his ambitions, Caesar moved quickly. Aided by Crassus and Pompey, he was elected Consul, the highest state office. Also with the help of his fellow triumvirs, he secured the passage of an agrarian law providing grants of land for 20,000 poor citizens and for Pompey's veterans. After some prolonged political maneuvering he also got himself appointed the rule of Cisalpine (Northern Italy) and Transalpine Gaul (roughly modern France, Switzerland, and the low countries) and Illyricum (roughly modern Yugoslavia) with four legions for five years (58 BC–54BC). His term of office was later extended to 49BC

RISE TO MILITARY GENIUS

In the years 58 BC to 49 BC Caesar conducted the Gallic campaigns revealing a military genius unrivaled in his, or most any other age. During these wars he very shrewdly used the leadership skill of *rhetoric* to shore up support back in Rome for his Gallic military campaigns. This was important not only for his personal reputation but also for ensuring a steady supply of goods and resources for his soldiers. Every great general must solve this political question of home-front support for the campaign. Caesar used rhetoric and political skill to do this.

He composed his literary masterpiece, the 'Commentaries' or the 'Gallic Wars', while actively conducting the wars the commentaries were describing. The commentaries were so well-written and described such an amazing series of military victories that his reputation in Rome as a first class General and conqueror was henceforth assured. As we mentioned above, the Commentaries were written essentially as dispatches sent back to Rome at regular intervals in order to spread news of his great victories. One would think therefore that they were mere propaganda in the modern sense designed to glorify Caesar by exaggerating his accomplishments and conquests. Historians, however, have found that the dispatches contained accounts of battles that were largely accurate and without exaggeration. Caesar, in fact, had no interest in spreading lies about his actions and accomplishments. It would have been nearly impossible, in any case, to do so given the number of people involved that regularly moved between Caesar's armies in Gaul and the Capitol in Rome.

Caesar's tactics in the Gallic wars repeatedly demonstrated his ability to dominate on the battlefield. We described many of Caesar's military victories in a previous chapter. Suffice it to say that he often won by outsmarting his enemy rather than outnumbering them. One of his favorite stratagems was the feint. He would send a small force against a larger enemy force which would then naturally be repulsed causing many of the enemy warriors to believe they had victory. Discipline and vigilance would then flag in the enemy camp giving Caesar his chance. Caesar would then pretend a strategic retreat from the field, thus luring the enemy armies into a vulnerable position between Caesar's flanks. This allowed an encircling maneuver by Caesar's armies, thus canceling the enemies' advantages in numbers.

With these sort of battlefield stratagems (supplemented by diplomatic skill) Caesar conquered all of Gaul against overwhelming odds. By the end of the Gallic wars Caesar had reduced all of Gaul to Roman control. In the course of the Gallic campaigns Caesar had fought at least 30 major battles, winning virtually all of them. He captured over 800 towns, over a million enemy soldiers and killed another million. He conquered an area twice the size of Italy itself with far more millions of people than the province of Spain. What is more, the lands were largely fertile and the towns potentially rich. Caesar's conquests turned the Roman Mediterranean Empire into a worldwide land empire. These Gallic campaigns proved him one of the greatest military commanders of all time.

ENEMIES BACK IN ROME

Caesar's military successes had aroused Pompey's concerns and perhaps his jealousy. The conservative Senate and Pompey realizing that Caesar had become too popular, too powerful, and too dangerous, made common cause against Caesar. When in 54 BC Julia, daughter of Caesar and wife of Pompey, died the personal and political ties between the two men began to weaken. Crassus' death (53 BC) in a disastrous military campaign against Parthia marked the end of the First Triumvirate.

THE ROAD TO THE RUBICON

Caesar hoped to be Consul again when his term in Gaul expired. Holding public office in Rome was all-important because it meant immunity from politically-motivated prosecution which, no matter how frivolous, could ruin even a powerful man. Caesar needed to return to Rome and hold office both to avoid such distractions and to work his will on Roman political and legal institutions. In order to clip Caesar's wings, the Senate demanded that Caesar give up his army and his appointment as Governor of Gaul *before* he took up office as Consul in Rome. Meeting these demands would make Caesar vulnerable to his most dangerous enemy: Pompey. In 50 BC, Caesar wrote the senate that he would give up his army if Pompey would give up his. The senate refused Caesar's compromise offer and now began the portentous events that led to the crossing of the Rubicon and civil war.

As the contest between the Senate and Caesar began to heat up, two tribunes faithful to Caesar, Marc Antony and Quintus Cassius Longinus fled to Caesar, who was encamped in Northern Italy before the Rubicon. Caesar began to assemble his armies in northern Italy and asked for the support of the soldiers against the senate. The army called for action. Caesar, for the first time in his life, hesitated. He had come to his moment of destiny.

WHY CAESAR HESITATED

Ancient law and custom decreed that no Roman general should take his armies across the Rubicon and threaten the city of Rome. Caesar could not legally return to the City unless he renounced his arms. On the other hand sans his armies he would be in the hand of his enemies in the senate and powerless against Pompey. In addition, his veterans would not be given the rewards due them for their service to Rome in hard-fought battles in Gaul. Finally, without his armies he could not adequately protect the people back in Rome who were his supporters.

If he disbanded his armies and entered Rome as a private citizen there was no guarantee that he would not be immediately proscribed by the Senate, thus giving Pompey a legal fig-leaf to go after all of Caesar's friends and relatives. He would very likely be immediately framed on some specious charge, executed or exiled, and his property confiscated —property he had just fought so hard for over seven years in Gaul.

On the other hand, he knew that if he did not disband his armies he faced certain Civil War and not with just any general, but with Pompey—a very capable man indeed. Pompey's conquests were as magnificent as Caesar's and perhaps more so because Pompey had accomplished most of his while he was still a young man. What is more is that Pompey with senatorial support had publicly boasted that he could raise an army far larger than what Caesar had at his disposal.–The prospect of facing Pompey, this very capable warrior on the battlefield, must have seemed daunting to Caesar. Add to it that this was the man who had cared genuinely for his (Caesar's) beloved daughter when the two were married (and she apparently genuinely loved Pompey in turn) it becomes clear that Caesar must at a minimum had at least some personal misgivings as to the course of action to take.

Added to all these largely personal concerns were considerations of what was best for Rome itself. We are licensed to believe that Caesar was more than just a mere opportunist—as he certainly tried to spare Rome a civil war by coming to terms with the Senate and with Pompey. Although we cannot describe them in detail here, negotiations between Caesar and the Senate/Pompey were in fact prolonged and serious—at least on Caesar's side. Caesar repeatedly offered compromise and the Senate repeatedly rejected compromise. In addition, when Caesar finally was able to rule Rome without substantial interference from the Senate he revealed a far-ranging vision for the re-organization of the empire, and restoration of political order. Indeed, it became clear that Caesar had plans for creation of a whole new world order, far beyond any plans for mere personal aggrandizement. Thus, he must have been thinking to some extent, not purely of his own narrow interests, but of Rome's interests as well and for Caesar, Rome's interests were synonymous with those of political Order itself. To the extent, therefore, that he saw his mission as the restoration of order in the Roman world, rather than mere accumulation of ever more personal power, Caesar must have weighed the choice before him (of whether or not to cross the Rubicon with an army) in terms of the consequences for world order.

What is more is that he could see before him the ruinous consequences of the mis-rule of Rome by his enemies in the Senate and by Pompey. Rome left to the rule of Pompey and the senate while Caesar was in Gaul fared badly. Although Pompey was a first rate warrior, he lacked political skill and the will to rule. Rome under his ineffectual leadership began to sink into political chaos and corruption. The Senate too could not, or would not act.

Neglect of sound administration of the provinces further tore at the weakened fabric of the republic. Rome's enemies, noting the chaos and internal conflict in the Capitol, sought to take military advantage of these internal divisions. Uprisings in the provinces started to occur and gangs of disgruntled 'citizens' began to roam the streets of all of the major cities including Rome itself, looting and terrorizing the citizens. Caesar must have deplored the sight after he had just restored order to Gaul. He must thus had asked himself whether he had a responsibility to cross the Rubicon with an army and restore order—yet all of tradition claimed that such a crossing was breaking the law and against the order of Rome.

Although Caesar knew that crossing the Rubicon would result in civil war and thus a short–term increase in the general disorder afflicting the state, he believed that if his luck held and he won the civil wars, the win would result in long-term benefits for Rome itself as well as a more stable political order for the world. He knew also that he had to act swiftly in order to forestall invasion by enemies of Rome seeking to take advantage of its internal disorders and weak leadership.

To achieve the rather lofty aims of restoration of political order and reorganization of the empire, Caesar had to risk his life and perhaps those of all of his friends and relatives. He knew better than anyone else that the odds of winning a series of pitched military battles against Pompey, who had all the resources of the State behind him, were slim indeed. Yet, as far as he was concerned, if he did not act, Rome would sink into further political chaos On the other hand if he did act, he would probably be defeated, and he and those under his protection would all be executed and Rome would then be fully in the hands of Pompey and the Senate, with disastrous political consequences for the state. It is no wonder that Caesar hesitated.

But he did not hesitate for long and he did not despair. He rapidly came to a decision. Indeed he gave every indication of not only *not* shrinking from the battle ahead of him but of actually relishing the coming fight. In coming to such a momentous decision when all that was dear to him hung in the balance, he drew on the one thing necessary for great leadership and success—his audacity of spirit. His unshakeable belief in his destiny allowed him to discard with contempt any further considerations of caution and discretion. Like that mad lover whom we call God, or the Fates, Caesar would gamble everything on a throw of the dice— trusting in his own greatness of spirit to carry him through. He called upon that great character, formed steadily in all of his past struggles and which now revealed itself in the relish with which he threw caution to the wind, allowing instead his fearlessness and rage to fuse with his innate and caustic, audacity of spirit, to come finally to his decision: He would fight!

CAESAR ACTS

On January 19, 49 BC, Caesar with the words *Iacta alea est* (the die is cast) crossed the Rubicon. He moved with lightning speed. This was not a man in a defensive posture!

He almost recklessly moved out ahead of the main body of his troops as if he was in pursuit of his foes rather then they of him! He had become an avenging angel. What is most amazing to historians ever since is that Caesar's foes actually turn tailed and ran! Attempts to rationalize the retreat of the forces of the Senate and of Pompey have included the fact that Pompey was ill with the flu, that he wanted to do battle with Caesar in Asia Minor where he (Pompey) had plenty of supplies and friends and so forth…but all of these explanations fail, as the retreat was a major blunder from any point of view you care to take. It allowed Caesar to march to Rome as its savior and protector. It allowed him while in Rome to pass legislation that legitimized/legalized his actions and to raise more resources and forces.

Once he restored order to the city of Rome Caesar proceeded to Brundisium, where he besieged Pompey until Pompey once again fled (March, 49 BC) with his fleet to Greece. Instead of immediately dealing with Pompey, Caesar set out at once for Spain, which Pompey's legates were holding, and pacified that province. Returning to Rome, Caesar held the dictatorship for 11 days in early December, long enough to get himself re-elected Consul, and then set out for Greece in pursuit of Pompey.

Caesar collected at Brundisium a small army and fleet. Characteristically for Caesar, he moved with lighting speed ahead of the bulk of his troops and slipped across a strait in pursuit of Pompey. He met Pompey at Dyrrhachium but, given his small army, he was forced to fall back and begin a long retreat southward, with Pompey in pursuit. Near Pharsalus, however, Caesar camped in a very strategic location and lured Pompey into an engagement on grounds favorable to Caesar. Pompey, who had a far larger army, attacked Caesar but was routed (48 BC) and fled to Egypt, where he was killed by the Egyptian Pharaoh. Caesar was thus left in sole command of Rome.

We will not go into the further history of Caesar, though it is fascinating. Read Plutarch's account of Caesar's affair with Cleopatra and how he established her firmly on the Egyptian throne; of his campaigns in Syria and Pontus, where he defeated (47 BC) Pharnaces II with such ease that he reported his victory in the words *Veni, vidi, vici* (I came, I saw, I conquered); or, finally, of his campaign in North Africa whither the followers of Pompey and the Senate were led by Cato. Caesar begged Cato to come over to his side, to become Consul and to assist Caesar in restoring Rome to its greatness. Cato refused to assist what he saw as a tyrant and, at the last, took his own life.

Returning to Rome as tribune of the people and dictator, Caesar surprised everyone by pardoning all his enemies. This further suggests that he was, indeed, interested in restoring order to Rome rather than mere personal aggrandizement. He set about reforming the living conditions of the people by passing agrarian laws and by improving housing accommodations. He also drew up the elaborate plans (which the Emperor Augustus later implemented with great success) for consolidating the empire and establishing it securely.

After putting down the last remnants of resistance led by Pompey's sons in Spain in 44 BC Caesar returned to Rome and became dictator for life. This move smacked of hubris and aroused great resentment among his enemies and especially in the Senate. Here Caesar's leadership skills finally failed him as he did not effectively manage the envy of his followers and friends.

The conspiracy to assassinate Caesar included certain of his friends and protégés, among them Cassius, and Marcus Junius Brutus—the son of his favorite mistress, Servilia. On March 15 (the Ides of March) of 44 BC, he was stabbed to death in the senate house. All of his murderers were later killed in battle or rounded up and executed by the Emperor Augustus.

This short summary of Caesar's life as told by Plutarch clearly demonstrates that he was a man who could and did combine both the prestige and the dominance styles of leadership. We believe that that flexibility, that ability to employ both strategies effectively and appropriately contributed to his military and political successes. He was certainly one of the greatest leaders of all time. During his later career he obviously did not manage his enemies well. Perhaps hubris caught up with him as it did with Alexander before him. Success after success leads to recklessness and arrogance. Like Alexander before him Caesar was making plans for further military conquest when he was cut down by death. Despite his untimely death Caesar had managed to put in place the basic institutional and legal arrangements that would later help Octavian usher in the golden age of Rome. Alexander too had done the same. It is remarkable how similar the two men were. We will consider Alexander's life next and conclude that Caesar was the greater leader and man.

Chapter 10

ALEXANDER: THE SYNTHESIS OF PRESTIGE AND DOMINANCE II

INTRODUCTION

At age 33 a man lay dying in a remote part of the ancient East. His death is note-worthy, for he was, in the opinion of many of his followers, the son of God. His life marks a transition from one age to another, a transition that even now, more than 2,000 years later, we note. That man was Alexander; inevitably styled *The Great.*

Alexander was born in 356 BC son of Philip II, king of Macedonia, one of the less glorious, but nevertheless important, outposts of Hellenic civilization. The Hellenes, that is the Greeks, had, for centuries, flourished on the islands of the Aegean, the seacoast of Asia Minor, and the mainland of Greece, including that remote northern region known as Macedonia. The Greeks had, also for centuries, nervously eyed their rival, the mighty Persian Empire that controlled the world east of the Bosporus.

Persia had tried, in 490 BC to invade and conquer Greece but was repulsed by the Athenians at Marathon. Later, in 401 BC a Greek expeditionary force of 10,000 marched into the heart of the Persian Empire and defeated the world's largest army; but they, too, quickly retreated to their homeland. So things continued for centuries as a sometimes hot, sometimes cold, war marked East-West relations.

Then came Alexander who changed everything. He subdued Greece and conquered all Persia. When Alexander died in 323 BC there was no Persian Empire remaining. Historians also mark, with Alexander's death, the end of the Hellenic epoch. Alexander's conquests in the West and the East united all of the known world in one new Hellenistic civilization that stretched from Europe and North Africa to India.

Alexander's conquests forever changed the world. Hellenistic civilization spread western science, philosophy, political theory, inquisitiveness, and rationality. The Hellenistic conquest remade every local culture it encountered. And we today, heirs of that Western Tradition, live in a world largely shaped by the Hellenistic world that Alexander inaugurated.

How could Alexander dare so great an undertaking --conquering an empire of the entire known world? What gave him the gall, the bravery, the smarts, the audacity, to do that?

Plutarch, our ancient guide thought he knew the answer to that question. While other ancient writers tell us merely of Alexander's mighty and marvelous deeds; only Plutarch gives us the early life of Alexander, the influences in Alexander's life, and crucially, he shows us the character of the man.

Plutarch opens his Life of Alexander by stating:

> It must be borne in mind that my design is not to write histories, but lives. And the most glorious exploits do not always furnish us with the clearest discoveries of virtue or vice in men; sometimes a matter of less moment, an expression or a jest, informs us better of their characters and inclinations, than the most famous sieges, the greatest armaments, or the bloodiest battles whatsoever.

So let us follow Plutarch, for a little while, as he paints a word portrait of Alexander, a man grappling with a unique destiny. The analogy is apt, for Plutarch himself records of his method:

> Therefore as portrait-painters are more exact in the lines and features of the face in which the character is seen, than in the other parts of the body, so I must be allowed to give my more particular attention to the marks and indications of the souls of men, and while I endeavor by these to portray their lives, may be free to leave more weighty matters and great battles to be treated of by others.

As we have pointed out in previous chapters, Plutarch claimed that the best road to eminence, leadership and greatness is via emulation of a worthy model, so it is not surprising that Alexander had three heroes he tried to emulate:

> --*Achilles*, the legendary hero of Homer's Iliad, Alexander's favorite book;
> --*Hercules*, whose superhuman deeds Alexander often invoked when addressing his men before battle; and
> --*Cyrus the Great*, the Persian king.

Education also recurs as a theme in Plutarch's life of Alexander. Again, in our earlier chapters we established the importance of education in the development of leadership traits. Interestingly, Plutarch does not rank birth (that is one parents), wealth, or location (coming from a famous city) nearly as highly as he places education when it comes to character formation. When Plutarch writes of Caius Marius, one of Rome's greatest military leaders and an inspiration for Julius Caesar, he tells us that Marius, for all his incomparable actions in battle, ultimately wrecked himself and ended his years in cruelty and vindictiveness because his passions had never been tamed by a liberal education (Life of Marius, 2).

Of Alexander's education what can we say, but that he had the finest available anywhere in the world in his time, or most any time? His teacher was Aristotle, perhaps the widest ranging thinker in human history.

Alexander was, Plutarch tells us, "naturally a great lover of all kinds of learning and reading." (Life of Alexander, 8) Like Patton, Robert E. Lee, and other great generals, when on military campaign Alexander slept with a dagger and copy of Homer's *Iliad* under his pillow. He said that with these two close by he was prepared for come what may. Alexander was also a devoted reader of the great dramatists of the Hellenic world --Euripides, Sophocles, and Aeschylus-- and other Greek authors.

Love of learning, however, is not enough. Plutarch argued that you also need a passion for distinction, glory, and honor. Alexander was naturally ambitious. With each victory won by his father Philip, Alexander sees a lost opportunity for Alexander. He was resolved to conquer, not merely inherit, his kingdom. He was the son of the king of a nation that was on the ascendancy. And he had, as we noted, the best possible education. But there were many young ambitious noblemen with money and education, but only one Alexander the Great. What made Alexander, *The Great*?

From his reading, Alexander must have felt he had actually come to know his models: Hercules, Achilles, and Cyrus the Great. That final choice is striking. After all, it was Alexander's defeat of a later Persian king that marks him as the first world (as opposed to local territorial) conqueror. The habits of the mind, developed in Alexander by his tutors and his reading, prepared him to seek the best models wherever they may be found. And he found that model in a foreigner --a barbarian!

To be sure, when the Greeks said "barbarian" they merely meant "non-Greek." Still, the choice of Cyrus as a model is curious. Now, after Homer, Alexander's favorite author was Xenophon the Athenian. Xenophon wrote a treatise the Education of Cyrus (or *Cyropaediea*) that was a kind of how-to book on kingship. Xenophon portrays Cyrus as the ideal warrior and statesmen --a just and magnanimous conqueror who administered the empire he conquered for the most part with wisdom, tolerance and justice.

Picture Alexander, one day at the height of his military accomplishments in the heart of Persia: hot, tired, sweaty, after lightning-swift conquests in Persia. He first rewards his faithful men with portions of the booty. He next looks to his newly acquired Persian subjects and begins to take on the locally expected duties of the king. But then his thoughts bend to his model, Cyrus. He makes a pilgrimage to the tomb of Cyrus the Great who died in 529 BC, two centuries before the birth of Alexander. Finding the tomb had been vandalized he executes the Macedonian who defiled the tomb of the Great barbarian King. He has the monument painstakingly rebuilt (by his best Architect Aristobulos) and watched over by the local satrap and the proper religious authorities, the magi and priests who were to perform perpetual sacrifices for Cyrus. Can there be any better evidence for his reverence for the person he hoped to emulate?

Before battle, Alexander would also invoke the memory of the legendary deeds of the demi-god Hercules. Alexander, in fact, claimed that he descended from Hercules. He lived in an age when such claims were the ticket to fame, not the nut house. Perhaps he really believed it. We do know that he had silver coins struck depicting himself as Hercules. Now that's audacity of spirit! An audacity that goes deep to one's bedrock belief system about the Self: I am not just any mortal: I am like Cyrus and Hercules!

Finally, Alexander looked to the Greek hero Achilles, as celebrated in Homer's epic poem. From Achilles Alexander learned to conquer fear, embrace danger, disregard death, and seek the immortality of fame and conquest. He also learned a lesson in friendship and partnership.

In short, Alexander had big ambitions and a passion for distinction. Alexander early on showed signs of his later greatness. In the familiar story of Alexander's taming of the wild horse Bucephelus (Life of Alexander, 9), Alexander's audacity propels him toward his future greatness. He believed in his abilities, and his belief was well-founded, as he had prepared himself for greatness. Here Alexander's love of reading 'stands him in good stead' again. It turns out that Xenophon also wrote a treatise on horsemanship. From that treatise Alexander learned just as it is wise to *not* to antagonize loyal subjects with onerous decrees, so too it is wise to avoid threats and violence when breaking in a new mount. This insight served him well in a now famous passage from Plutarch.

> Philonicus the Thessalian brought the horse Bucephalus to Philip, offering to sell him for thirteen talents; but when they went into the field to try him, they found him so very vicious and unmanageable, that he reared up when they endeavored to mount him, and would not so much as endure the voice of any of Philip's attendants. Upon which, as they were leading him away as wholly useless and intractable.
>
> Alexander, who stood by, said, "What an excellent horse do they lose, for want of address and boldness to manage him!" Philip at first took no notice of what he said; but when he heard him repeat the same thing several times, and saw he was much vexed to see the horse sent away, "Do you reproach," said he to him, "those who are older than yourself, as if you knew more, and were better able to manage him than they?"
>
> "I could manage this horse," replied Alexander, "better than others do." "And if you do not," said Philip, "what will you forfeit for your rashness?" "I will pay," answered Alexander, "the whole price of the horse." At this the whole company fell a laughing; and as soon as the wager was settled amongst them, he immediately ran to the horse, and taking hold of the bridle, turned him directly towards the sun, having, it seems, observed that he was disturbed at and afraid of the motion of his own shadow.
>
> Then letting him go forward a little, still keeping the reins in his hand, and stroking him gently when he found him begin to grow eager and fiery, he let fall his upper garment softly, and with one nimble leap securely mounted him, and when he was seated, by little and little drew in the bridle, and curbed him without either striking or spurring him. Presently, when he found him free from all rebelliousness, and only impatient for the course, he let him go at full speed, inciting him now with a commanding voice, and urging him also with his heel.

Philip and the crowd of onlookers called Alexander's wager "rash" and even a bit disrespectful to the adults who were responsible for the horse. We might call Alexander's wager audacious. Note that it was not uncommon for the young and inexperienced to be thrown from an untamable mount and even be seriously injured and shamed in the process. These considerations were nothing to the young Alexander who apparently saw in the horse something of his destiny.

To the amazement of all Alexander was able to mount the charger. Philip beaming with pride thereupon settled the bet and gave Bucephalus to Alexander. Bucephalus would accompany Alexander throughout all of his major campaigns. For the rest of the horse's life none but Alexander could mount Bucephalus. Legend has it that Bucephalus would always lower his body to help Alexander mount but buck wildly if anybody else tried to mount him. They also relate that Bucephalus would become monstrous and fearless when attacking enemies of Alexander's armies. Could it be that Bucephalus helped Alexander win some of his victories? When Bucephalus finally died at 30 (at Taxila in India), Alexander fell into a prolonged period of grief that only the mortal threat of war pulled him out of.

Alexander was the son of King Philip; that put him in line for serious consideration to become the next king, but he had to earn the position by boldness and success in battle and by leading his people. Frequently there were contests among contenders for the throne. It was during just one such crisis of succession, when two sons of the recently deceased king of Persia contended for the throne, that the Greeks in 401 BC invaded Persia planning to effect a regime change.

At the age of sixteen Alexander was made commander (they grew up fast in those days) in Macedonia during Philip's absence and quelled a rising of the hill-tribes on the northern border. Alexander so impressed his father that Philip later put him in charge of a company during a major battle—a battle that would pretty much settle the supremacy of Macedonians over all Greece. This was the battle at Chaeronea where Thebans and the Athenians marched out to meet Philip's armies in 338. Alexander headed the charge which broke the offensive of the 'Sacred Band'--a group of Theban warriors who had never been defeated in battle. Philip, through a feigned retreat, lured the Athenians into the open and then defeated them in a pitched battle.

The next series of events cumulated rapidly and forever changed the life of Alexander and the world. In 337 BC Philip of Macedon, continuing a long pattern of marital infidelity, repudiated Alexander's mother Olympias for another wife. At a dinner celebrating the new marriage, the father of the bride made a toast wishing the couple 'many male heirs' to the kingdom. This toast was made in front of Alexander. In a rage Alexander threw his cup at the toaster thus insulting both Philip's guests and Philip himself. Alexander and a group of his loyal comrades were banished from the court for some time while his mother tried to patch up relations between Alexander and his father. Later Alexander discovered that negotiations were in progress between Philip and a neighboring kingdom with a view to effecting yet another marriage alliance that could imperil Alexander's succession. In short, Alexander kept receiving signs that his succession was no longer guaranteed.

In 336 Philip was assassinated while celebrating the marriage of his daughter. Representatives from all the Greek world were there and witnessed the killing but could not stop the lone assailant. This dramatic and searing tragedy precipitated Alexander's moment of destiny. However estranged from his father, he must have been appalled and outraged at his bloody murder. On the other hand, the sudden death of Philip presented Alexander with the opportunity to step in and seize the kingdom.

Was the assassin a lone nut or part of a conspiracy? We'll never know. And if a conspiracy, of whom? Philip's spurned wife, Alexander's mother, certainly had motives. The murder of Philip may have been conceived both as revenge of the slights of Olympias in favor of a new bride and the opportunity to put Philip away before sons from the new marriage could challenge Alexander's right to the throne. Alexander himself was suspected. Ultimately, we'll never know who was behind the plot.

There was, in any case, no time to lose. Someone would be the new king. As far as Alexander was concerned it had to be Alexander. Surely the other contenders for the throne would quickly murder Alexander if he did not act. So, for Alexander it was kill or be killed; act or be acted upon. Besides concern for his own life, he had plans for Macedonia and dreams for the world. Only Alexander knew that Macedonia could, and under him would, rule all of Greece and liberate the Greece cities in Asia Minor.

The young Alexander, aged only 20, acted swiftly to secure the support of the army and soon swept all rivals for the throne from his path. The assassin was captured but conveniently murdered before he could talk and implicate anyone in the plot. Alexander had Philip's newborn son (by his recent bride) put to death. He also ordered the death of his cousin Amyntas, another potential claimant to the throne, following the brutal, but at the time quite normal, principle that a king who leaves no rivals lives to enjoy the kingship.

Alexander was, at this time, undisputed ruler of Macedonia, a fairly important local kingdom with control of major parts of the Greek peninsula. At the news of Philip's death, most of Greece rose in revolt against the Macedonians. Alexander, as Cyrus earlier and Caesar later, then moves with lighting speed, he acts with brash audacity, taking over 'commands' of various armies even when none were offered, concentrating available military forces, and then acting decisively with overwhelming might, surprise and command.

His 'forced march' from the North took the Thebans completely by surprise, and in a few days the city was taken. Whereas in the previous war with Thebes and Athens, Philip had spared the two cities, Alexander decided to use Thebes to make a statement. He wanted no uprisings and unrest while he was gone from the mainland on his Persian campaigns. Thebes was therefore utterly destroyed—an object lesson for the rest of the Greeks. (Characteristically, Alexander spared the city's temples and the house which had belonged to the poet Pindar).

Alexander's sense of reverence and proportion, and his human feeling, were restraints on his warlike temper that appear again and again in his life. His ability to put himself in the place of his fellow man served him well as a leader, as in this episode related by Plutarch.

While they were in this distress, it happened that some Macedonians who had fetched water in skins upon their mules from a river they had found out, came about noon to the place where Alexander was, and seeing him almost choked with thirst, presently filled a helmet and offered it him. He asked them to whom they were carrying the water; they told him to their children, adding, that if his life were but saved, it was no matter for them, they should be able well enough to repair that loss, though they all perished. Then he took the helmet into his hands, and looking round about, when he saw all those who were near him stretching their heads out and looking, earnestly after the drink, he returned it again with thanks without tasting a drop of it, "For," said he, "if I alone should drink, the rest will be out of heart" (Life of Alexander, 42).

His reading of the life of Cyrus taught Alexander that enemies must be first defeated; then befriended. This helped assure that they will not rise against you later.

CROESUS, CYRUS AND ALEXANDER

Alexander certainly knew the story--it was a favorite in the ancient world-- of Croesus, a man famed for his wealth, hence the saying "rich as Croesus," who found himself on the wrong side of his lord Cyrus. When Croesus saw that capture was inevitable he prepared, in the age-old Asiatic custom, to destroy himself, his household, and his treasures in a huge funeral pyre (some stories have it that Cyrus had ordered the pyre as punishment). Croesus then tells Cyrus a moral tale that Solon the wisest of the Greeks had told him to the effect that wisdom, not riches and possession make for enduring happiness. Cyrus, impressed with the lesson, prevented the fire and convinced Croesus to become his friend and faithful adviser (Life of Solon, 28).

After Alexander defeated Cyrus's successor, Darius, he controlled conquered peoples far more numerous than the Greeks. Having won the war, how could he keep the peace with resentful subjects? Alexander's solution was to treat them not as conquered enemy, but as potential allies. In many ways Alexander adopted Persian manners and customs. This made it easier for the Persians to see Alexander as the new Persian ruler, not as a detested conquering Greek.

His Greek compatriots did not like these manners, claiming they were pompous and not fit for free men. Alexander argued that they were the only means to effectively govern the Persian masses. He sought ways to merge the Grecian and oriental cultures. He even staged a weeklong celebration of hundreds of marriages between his top soldiers and local Persian princesses and nobility. Integration of his followers into one united body via inter-marriage is an example of using a prestige strategy to rule. Force and dominance are eschewed in favor of cultural and religious links between the leader and the led between the rulers and the ruled. Greek resistance to "barbarian" ways was even stronger than Alexander anticipated, and his attempted melting pot was of only partial success. Still, it shows that he was, at the height of his success, striving to make his new conquest stable.

Alexander further showed his administrative genius and his ability to synthesize the two leadership styles (prestige and dominance) in exotic Egypt. Like Cyrus the Great, Alexander knew that it was much wiser to turn old or potential enemies into friends by treating them well and by giving them an interest in your goals and success. To win over the conquered Egyptians Alexander sacrificed piously to the gods of Memphis and began to meet with all of the major Egyptian notables. We see this as an example of Alexander employing a prestige strategy in order to hold the leadership reins in Egypt. Essentially he says 'You can trust me as I am a pious and religious man. I will not rule by brute force.' He left the basic Egyptian administrative apparatus intact and confirmed many of the Egyptian priests and elites in their positions. The support for Alexander in Egypt remained firm throughout his campaigning.

Of course, most of Alexander's public life is filled with glorious battles from which Alexander emerges as world ruler. Plutarch's Life of Alexander, however, *attempts to capture the character behind these battles* and that will be out focus here. We'll touch on just a few highlights that illustrate principles of leadership.

Alexander had conquered all of Greece and was now turning his sights to liberation of Greek cities under Persian domination and then to conquering Persia itself.

He revived the Panhellenic alliance. He put his companions, who had stood by him when he was exiled following his falling-out with this father, in positions of command.

In the spring of 334, Alexander crossed over to Asia Minor with an army of between 30,000 and 40,000 men. He first visited the site of Troy and there paid his respects to his hero Achilles. He then set out on his conquest of Asia.

In preliminary battles against the frontier troops of the Persians Alexander developed a technique he was to use over and over again with devastating effect. Using feints and deceptive tactics Alexander would get the enemy to weaken the center of its lines. Alexander would then throw his major shock troops and cavalry against the center. Typically Alexander himself would ride at the head of this attack and head straight for the enemy's commander behind the centerlines.

THE BATTLE OF ISSUS (333 BC)

Alexander now turned his armies to face the best Persian fighters under the command of King Darius. This bold act surprised Darius. He was not expecting audacity! The Persians had a huge numerical advantage. Darius had taken months to raise this army of about 100,000. Alexander had only 30,000-40,000 men.

Now Alexander carefully scrutinized the Persian ranks arrayed against him. He noticed that Darius placed his young recruits and his archers on the left. This was a weakness in Darius massive armies and Alexander determined to take advantage of it. He therefore ordered his cavalry to focus its attack on this weak spot. As Darius left flank began to weaken Alexander led the bulk of his phalanxes along with his companion cavalry into the center of the Persian line. Alexander spotted the Persian king's chariot and he headed straight for it bearing down on it with an almost supernatural fury. With both the Persian left flank and the center collapsing Persian resistance collapsed. Darius fled the field. Among the hostages taken were members of the Persian royal family including the mother of Darius, as well as his wives.

Soon thereafter Alexander received a letter from Darius seeking to ransom his family and claiming that Alexander was an aggressor and breaker of an old alliance between Philip and Persia. Alexander in reply said that he was avenging the wrong done to Greece by Xerxes and more recently by Ochus who had invaded the domain of his father Philip. He accused Darius of being behind the assassination of his father Philip. Alexander further instructed Darius that the royal family would be returned whenever Darius decided to come and ask in person.

After the battle of Issus, Alexander methodically began to occupy Syria and Phoenicia. The old general Parmenion was given the task of conquering through siege warfare the great city of Damascus. When it fell Damascus' immense treasure fell into Alexander's hands. The Great King's war chest was kept there and thus Alexander and his armies were rich beyond their wildest imaginations. Alexander no longer had to worry about financing his military campaigns.

Alexander later showed that he could deal quite severely with populations that obstinately resisted his armies. The conquest of the Phoenician coast was not to be altogether easy, for Tyre put up a spirited resistance and for seven months Alexander had to lay siege to it. When it fell, Alexander dealt severely with Tyrian people. He allowed 30,000 of them to be sold as slaves.

At some time during the Tyrian siege another embassy from Darius was received. Darius now offered an immense sum as ransom for his family as well as a partition of his empire. Darius was ready to cede the bulk of his empire to Alexander in exchange for peace. Darius also offered an alliance and his daughter's hand in marriage.

The old general Parmenion said to Alexander "I'd accept the offer if I were you." Whereupon Alexander replied, *"If I were you, so would I. But I am Alexander!"*

Alexander sent message back to Darius that he already possessed Darius' former empire and could take Darius daughter to wife anytime he pleased. If Darius wanted an alliance let him come to Alexander and plead his case!

The occupation of the rest of Syria and Palestine proceeded smoothly, and after the fall of Gaza Alexander's way lay open into Egypt. Even Alexander's great model Cyrus the Great had never conquered Egypt. Alexander's reputation won Egypt without a fight.

Before leaving Egypt to complete his conquest of Persia Alexander traveled to the oracle of Zeus Ammon. It is said that there he got the answer he had been seeking, the confirmation of earlier rumors and speculation. He was, the oracle is supposed to have said, the son of the Great God Zeus.

Alexander, in his conquests, had already surpassed the territorial holdings of his father and of his model, Cyrus the Great. He had surpassed every man in courage, stamina, daring and success. This young man who had known only five or so years earlier only the meager and rustic environs of Macedonia now commanded whole nations. He was wealthy beyond the capacity of any Greek to imagine. He held absolute power over millions of lives, thousands of cities and dozens of nations. Two weeks before his visit to the Shrine he was made Pharaoh of all Egypt, undergoing the ancient rites of the Egyptians before hundreds of thousands of retainers. Another example of the subtle use of the prestige strategy to maintain rule and order over a conquered people. A few months before the Egyptian ceremonies he had essentially taken possession of the Persian Empire. Aside from some mopping up operations with respect to the remnants of Darius' armies, there seemed nothing in the known world left to conquer. This young man is then told by an Oracle of Zeus that he is divine. Could any of us have resisted the pull into hubris at this point?

Alexander began to treat his life as a mission and a destiny. The old Alexander began to recede and the new Alexander, Ruler of the Known World, began to appear. Henceforth all of his major actions would be accompanied by astrological signs and portents that the ancients took all too seriously and presumably so did Alexander.

BATTLE OF GUAGAMELA (331 BC)

In the spring of 331 Alexander could at last leave the Mediterranean and turn to eliminating Darius and the remnants of the Persian resistance. It was near Arbela and the village Guagamela that Alexander's armies met the armies of the great King. Darius had, in fact, in a last ditch effort, amassed between 50,000 and 100,000 soldiers and was waiting to engage Alexander on the central plains near Guagamela. A lunar eclipse fixes the exact date, September 20, 331 BC, as the day upon which the Macedonian army crossed the river Tigris. Alexander's men took the eclipse as a negative sign but Alexander took it as confirmation that he would once again win and win decisively.

When the two armies met Alexander very quickly sized up the situation. The flat plains gave the Persian army an advantage because they had use of the most modern weaponry, chariots that carried blades to slice through his warriors. Alexander lured Darius to attack the Macedonian center by making it appear to be weak. Darius fell for the trick and his armies broke through and even began to sack the Macedonian camps behind the lines. While the Persians, thinking themselves the victors, were thus occupied, Alexander's reserves attacked from their rear and annihilated the first wave of Persian forces. Then Alexander employed a second line of heavy infantry behind the front line to encircle the Persians. Alexander had his troops advance in an oblique diamond shaped formation against Darius' left flank. This maneuver confused the Persian commanders luring them into an attempt to encircle the Macedonian left flank. This further weakened their central lines. Now Alexander went after the Persian center and Darius himself. The Persian lines quickly collapsed and Darius once again fled. This time his own soldiers had had enough of the incompetent King and they killed him.

The rest of the story in Persia is simply one of a triumphal progression through the empire. At Ecbatana, (near modern day Teheran) the beautiful summer residence of the Persian nobility, new masses of treasure were seized.

Alexander had, by the winter of 329-328 reached the Kabul valley at the foot of the Hindu Kush. He now began to conceive plans to invade and conquer India.

One of the problems every leader has to face is how to win followers to your way of looking at things. How do you convince your followers to go along with your vision and plans? Which strategy do you use, coercion/dominance or persuasion/prestige?

In the case of Alexander he used both.. but only after making a few colossal mistakes. He was ready to press into India, they wanted to settle down and enjoy the considerable wealth they had captured already. He needed to govern the Persian Empire which expected a king to act like, well, a king, even like a god. They were Macedonian Greeks who violently resisted any form of tyranny.

At banquet one night Cleitus the Black, a man who had saved Alexander's life in a former battle, accused Alexander to his face of becoming too Persian, of acting as a despot instead of a leader. Everyone there, including Alexander, was quite drunk on wine. Alexander took up a spear and killed Cleitus on the spot. When he sobered up, they say, he later bitterly regretted this drunken behavior.

To begin the campaign in India Alexander put two of his closest associates (Perdiccas and Hephestion, with him since the days of the exile in Epirus) in charge of the heavier troops and had them all move down the Kabul valley to Pencelaotis. Alexander with a body of lighter-armed troops and cavalry pushed up the valleys. At one point Alexander and his men had to storm a stronghold of a fierce people perched on a precipitous summit above the Indus, which it was said that Hercules himself had failed to take. When Alexander accomplished the feat he once again surpassed in glory and exploit one of his major heroes.

Meanwhile Perdiccas and Hephaestion had built a bridge over the Indus, and by this in the spring of 326 Alexander's armies passed into the Punjab region between the Indus and the Hydaspes, in a region centered in the great city of Taxila.

Unlike many of the other local warlords who were frightened, King Porus prepared to fight Alexander. The two armies met across the river Hydaspes. It was a most awesome battle. When it finally became clear that the Macedonians had won the day, Porus himself fell sorely wounded and was brought to Alexander. In his usual manner, Alexander treated the wounded warrior with dignity and asked Porus to be his friend! Alexander put Porus in charge of the entire region he had conquered in India and thus the two became steadfast friends.

After this victory Alexander was eager for new conquests but now his men finally began to baulk. The Macedonian army refused to go any farther. As one historian put it: "It was a bitter mortification to Alexander, before whose imagination new vistas had just opened out eastwards, where there beckoned the unknown world of the Ganges and its splendid kings. For three days the will of king and people were locked in antagonism; then Alexander gave way; the long eastward movement was ended; the return began".

He could no longer rely on only a single strategy-that of dominance. He as born a King and was used to people doing his will. Without an army however he as nothing and thus he had to listen to the wishes of his army and they insisted on a behavior change in their leader....They wanted more persuasion and less domination. Alexander slowly began to use the prestige option more and more after the confrontation with his troops in India.

Although he had agreed to return to Persia with his armies, Alexander got his soldiers to agree to return by a route unknown to the Greeks. He wanted to explore the routes between India and Persia. He set out to explore the great river Hydaspes to its mouth. The fleet governed by Nearchus prepared on the Hydaspes sailed in October, while a land army moved along the bank. The confluence of the Hydaspes and Acesines passed, the Macedonians were once more in a region of hostile tribes with towns to be stormed. It was at one of these, a town of the Malli, that a memorable incident occurred, such as characterized the personality of Alexander for all succeeding time. He leapt from the wall with only three companions into the hostile town, and, before the army behind him could effect an entrance, lay wounded almost to death. Here was a case of crossing the line between audaciousness and recklessness. Alexander's bravery knew no bounds. By this brash act he not only endangered himself but also his men who had to follow after him to protect him.

He recovered and beat down the resistance of the tribes along the river route, leaving them annexed to the Macedonian satrapy west of the Indus. Back in Persia Alexander turned his attention to governance. He vigorously pursued his policy of fusion of the two races Greek and Persians. He staged the great marriage festival at Susa, when he himself took two more wives from the Persian royal house, and married off a number of his generals to Oriental princesses, and even induced as many as he could of the rank-and-file to take Asiatic wives.

At Ecbatana in 326-325 Alexander lost his companion Hephestion. He ordered a huge burial service. His architects built such a large funeral pyre that it was considered an architectural wonder of the world. No expense was spared in the funeral rites and all the world waited for Alexander to emerge from his mourning. War and battle brought him back to life. In the winter (324-323) he was again active, bringing the hill- tribes on the border of Media into subjection.

He next planned a huge military and exploratory expedition to northern Europe. Before he could complete these plans he developed fever; lingered for a few weeks and then died. He was only 33 years old.

There was no Alexander II waiting to take control of the empire after Alexander's death. As we all learned in school, his empire was divided among his generals and it was not until centuries had passed and the Roman Empire wrested control of nearly all of the old Alexandrian empire (along with many lands in the west and north than Alexander never dreamed of) did another unified state control so large a swath of the earth as did Alexander. But line-of-succession is not the sole test of continuity of Alexander's conquests.

We have maintained in this monograph that central role of a leader is to create ordered society. How does Alexander fare by that criterion?

After conquering Egypt without the need of fighting a single battle, Alexander founded the city of Alexandria. This Hellenistic settlement at the mouth of the Nile would grow to become a great cosmopolitan center. The city, with its famous library, was destined to be a center of learning, commerce and spiritual upheaval for centuries to come.

Alexander set up Greek schools in the conquered territories. His empire spread the Greek language and Greek thought. Although politically divided, the Hellenistic world that thrived for centuries after the death of Alexander (and of which we are the heirs) first propagated, and then maintained, a single civilization with the internal resources to adapted to local customs and thrive for centuries.

If we compare the leadership abilities of Alexander to those of Julius Caesar we must certainly call Caesar the greater man and leader. Alexander never had to report his actions to anyone like a Senate as did Caesar. Alexander was therefore accountable to no-one. Only under extreme conditions did his troops question him or dare to oppose his commands. While both men elicited almost fanatical loyalty from their soldiers Caesar appeared to retain that loyalty for a longer period of time than did Alexander. This is a remarkable fact as after he had conquered Persia Alexander commanded almost limitless financial resources so that he had little problem feeding his armies. Caesar on the other hand had to use very subtle, complex and ingenious political skills to obtain supplies for his men. Caesar had to cajole, threaten and push the Gallic tribes into providing resources. He had to use all of his political and rhetorical skills to get the Senate to continue to sanction his conquests in Gaul. Bribery helped as well. Caesar's Gallic commentaries are masterpieces of rhetoric and persuasion. These books helped Caesar win the propaganda campaign back home so that his military exploits could continue. Alexander faced no such challenges and therefore never really fully developed the prestige oriented style of leadership. Thus, with respect to the prestige strategy, Caesar wins hands down.

What about the comparison of military skills? Again we must give the prize to Caesar. While Alexander certainly very often faced overwhelming numbers in his opponents so did Caesar but Caesar did so under greater constraints than did Alexander. Caesar showed that he could defeat the enemy in both pitched battles and when the enemy used guerilla tactics. Alexander furthermore never appeared to have faced the situation of encirclement as did Caesar at Alesia. In this extraordinary battle Caesar won in an impossible situation. He did so by not panicking and by digging massive trenchworks all around his encampments. In other words Caesar mastered the details of technical warfare in a way that Alexander never did.

What about character? Here again Caesar wins over Alexander. Alexander allowed himself to succumb to the sin of hubris. He allowed himself to be assimilated into the 'divine kingship' in Egypt and in Persia. Caesar, on the other hand, never wholly gave himself over to hubris. There are signs that Alexander was really beginning to think of himself as a God after he had conquered Persia. Caesar, in taking on the role of lifelong Dictator, appeared to have wanted to use the power to effect radical political reforms. He was less interested in power for power's sake.

What preserves a leader from corruption then is the ability to synthesize the two forms of leadership style we have referred to throughout this book. Certainly intelligence helps one to accomplish the synthesis but intelligence is not enough. Cato was smart but could never master the dominance strategy at all. His puritanical stance did not prevent him from being vindictive and fanatically destructive to the interests of Rome. Judicious use of political coercion is sometimes called for –particularly when dealing with large scale chaotic situations.

So how then does one synthesize dominance and prestige; persuasion and coercion, liberality and firmness? Caesar's life suggests that what protects a leader from corruption and from the error of relying on one strategy over the other is possession of a strategic vision for the 'world'. A philosophy of life and death is crucial if a leader is to successfully order his energies and appetites. Caesar appeared to be working toward some over-riding goal in his life. That goal appeared to be one world order under Rome. Not just any order but a just order. He had concluded that Rome was the only chance for such a just and ordered commonwealth and thus he worked to realize that order. He was willing to do violence to achieve the order but not inordinate violence. His strategic vision or philosophy of Life acted to put constraints on his behaviors and guided his political and military strategies. He was able to order his priorities in terms of the overall vision of order under Rome and this in turn allowed him to synthesize the prestige and dominance leadership styles in such a way as to found a new civilization that would last a thousand years.

REFERENCES

Anderson, S. W., Bechara, A., Damasio, H., Tranel, D., and Damasio, A. R. (1999). Impairment of social and moral behavior related to early damage in human prefrontal cortex. *Nature Neuroscience, 2*(11), 1032-1037.

Antonakis, J., and Atwater, L. (2002). Leader distance: A review and a proposed theory. *The Leadership Quarterly: An International Journal of Political, Social and Behavioral Science, 13*(6), 673-704.

Austin, J. L. (1962). *How to do things with words.* Oxford: Clarendon Press.

Axelrod, R. (1984). *The evolution of cooperation.* New York: Basic Books.

Axelrod, R., and Hamilton, W. D. (1981). The evolution of cooperation. *Science, 211,* 1390-1396.

Banyas, C. A. (1999). Evolution and phylogenetic history of the frontal lobes. In B. L. Miller and J. L. Cummings (Eds.), *The human frontal lobes: functions and disorders* (pp. 83-106). New York: The Guilford Press.

Bara, B. G., Tirassa, M., and Zettin, M. (1997). Neuropragmatics: Neuropsychological constraints on formal theories of dialogue. *Brain and Language, 59,* 7-49.

Barkley, R. A. (1997). Behavioral inhibition, sustained attention, and executive functions: Constructing a unifying theory of ADHD. *Psychological Bulletin, 121*(1), 65-94.

Barrett, J., Richert, R., and Driesenga, A. (2001). God's beliefs versus mother's: The development of nonhuman agent concepts. *Child Development, 72,* 50-65.

Barton, R. A., and Dunbar, R. I. M. (1997). Evolution of the social brain. In A. Whiten and R. W. Byrne (Eds.), *Machiavellian intelligence II: Extensions and evaluations* (pp. 240-263). Cambridge: Cambridge University Press.

Bass, B. M. (1998). *Transformational leadership: Industrial, military, and educational impact.* Mahwah, NJ: Lawrence Erlbaum Associates.

Blair, R. J. R. (1997). Moral reasoning and the child with psychopathic tendencies. *Personality and Individual Differences, 22,* 731-739.

Blair, R. J. R. (1999). Psychophysiological responsiveness to the distress of others in children with autism. *Personality and Individual Differences, 26,* 477-485.

Boyd, R., and Richerson, P. J. (1988). The evolution of reciprocity in sizeable groups. *Journal of Thermal Biology, 132,* 337-356.

Brandt, H., Hauert, C., and Sigmund, K. (2003). Cooperation, punishment and reputation in spatial games. *Proceedings of the Royal Society of London, Series, B, 270,* 1099- 1104.

Brothers, L. A. (1999). A neuroscientific perspective on human sociality. In R. J. Russell, N. Murphy, T. C. Meyering, and M. A. Arbib (Eds.), *Neuroscience and the person: Scientific perspectives on divine action* (pp. 67-76). Vatican City State: Vatican Observatory Publications.

Burns, J. M. (1978). *Leadership*. New York: Harper and Row.

Byrne, R. W., and Whiten, A. (1988). Machiavellian intelligence: Social expertise and the evolution of intellect in monkeys, apes, and humans. Oxford: Oxford University Press.

Chartrand, T. L., and Bargh, J. A. (1999). The chameleon effect: The perception-behavior link and social interaction. *Journal of Personality and Social Psychology, 76*(6), 893-910.

Chen, G., Gully, SM., Whiteman, J and Kilcullen, RN. (2000). Examination of relationships among trait-like individual differences, state-like individual differences, and learning performance. *Journal of Applied Psychology*, 85, 835-847.

Chorney, M. J., Chorney, K., Seese, N., Owen, M. J., Daniels, J., McGuffin, P., et al. (1998). A quantitative trait locus (QTL) associated with cognitive ability in children. *Psychological Science, 9,* 1-8.

Clark, H. H. (1985). Language use and language users. In G. Lindzey, and E. Aronson (Eds.), *The handbook of social psychology* (3rd ed., Vol. 2, pp. 179-232). Reading MA: Addison-Wesley.

Clark, H. H. (1996). *Using language*. Cambridge: Cambridge University Press.

Clutton-Brock, T. H., and Parker, G. A. (1995). Punishment in animal societies. *Nature,373,* 209-216.

Cohen, P. R., and Levesque, H. J. (1990). Rational interaction as the basis for communication. In P. R. Cohen, J. Morgan, and M. E. Pollack (Eds.), *Intentions in communication* (pp. 221-256). Cambridge, MA: MIT Press.

Cohen, P. R., Morgan, J., and Pollack, M. E. (Eds.). (1990). *Intentions in communication.* Cambridge, MA: The MIT Press.

Conger, J. (1998). The dark side of leadership. In G. R. Hickman (Ed.), *Leading organizations: Perspectives for a new era* (pp. 250-260). London: SAGE.

Cowlishaw, G., and Dunbar, R. I. M. (1991). Dominance rank and mating success in male primates. *Animal Behavior, 41,* 1045-1056.

Damasio, A. (1996). *Descartes' error: Emotion, reason, and the human brain*. London: Papermac.

Damasio, A. R., Tranel, D., and Damasio, H. (1991). Individuals with sociopathic behavior caused by frontal damage fail to respond autonomically to social stimuli. *Behavioral Brain Research, 41,* 81-94.

Davidson, G. C., and Neale, J. M. (1994). *Abnormal psychology* (6th ed.). New York: John Wiley and Sons Pub.

Davies, M., and Stone, T. (1995). *Mental simulation*. Oxford: Blackwell Publishers.

Deckel, A. W., Hesselbrock, V., and Bauer, L. (1996). Antisocial personality disorder, childhood delinquency and frontal brain functioning: EEG and neuropsychological findings. *Journal of Clinical Psychology, 52,* 639-650.

Dessalles, J. –L. (1998). Altruism, status and the origin of relevance. In J. R. Hurford, M. Studdert-Kenedy, and C. Knight (Eds.), *Approaches to the evolution of language* (pp. 130-147). Cambridge: Cambridge University Press.

Durkheim, E. (1912/1995). *The elementary forms of religious life*. New York: The Free Press. (Original work published 1912)

Eisenberg, N., and Strayer, J. (1987). *Empathy and its development.* New York: Cambridge University Press.

Ellis, L. (1995). Dominance and reproductive success among nonhuman animals: A cross-species comparison. *Ethology and Sociobiology, 16,* 257-333.

Eslinger, P. J. (1998). Neurological and neuropsychological bases of empathy. *European Neurology, 39*(4), 193-199.

Fehr, E., and Gachter, S. (2002). Altruistic punishment in humans. *Nature, 415,* 137-140.

Gallese, V., Keysers, C., and Rizzolatti, G. (2004). A unifying basis of social cognition. *Trends in Cognitive Sciences, 8*(9), 396-403.

Gardner, H. (1995). *Leading minds: An anatomy of leadership.* New York: Basic Books.

Gibbs, R. W., Jr. (1999). *Intentions in the experience of meaning.* Cambridge: Cambridge University Press.

Gigerenzer, G. (1997). The modularity of social intelliegence. In A. Whiten and R. W. Byrne (Eds.), *Machiavellian intelligence II: Extensions and evaluations* (pp. 264-288). Cambridge: Cambridge University Press.

Grattan, L. M., Bloomer, R. H., Archambault, F. X., and Eslinger, P. J. (1994). Cognitive flexibility and empathy after frontal lobe lesion. *Neuropsychiatry, Neuropsychology and Behavioral Neurology, 7,* 251-259.

Greenleaf, R. K. (1996). *On becoming a servant leader.* San Francisco, CA: Jossey-Bass.

Grice, H. P. (1989). Studies in the way of words. Cambridge, MA: Harvard University Press.

Hauser, M. D. (1988). Invention and social transmission: New data from wild vervet monkeys. In R. W. Byrne and A. Whiten (Eds.), *Machiavellian intelligence: Social expertise and the evolution of intellect in monkeys, apes and humans* (pp. 327-343). Oxford: Clarendon Press.

Hauert, C., Haiden, N., and Sigmund, K. (2004). The dynamics of public goods. *DCDS-B,4*(3), 575-587.

Hauert, C., and Schuster, H. G. (1998). Extending the iterated prisoner's dilemma without synchrony. *Journal of Theoretical Biology, 192,* 155-166.

Hauert, C., and Szabó, G. (2003). Prisoner's dilemma and public goods games in different geometries: Compulsory versus voluntary interactions. *Complexity, 8,* 31-38.

Henrich, J., and Gil-White, F. J. (2001). The evolution of prestige. *Evolution and Human Behaviour, 22,* 165-196.

Humphrey, N. K. (1976). The social function of intellect. In P. P. G. Bateson and R. A. Hinde (Eds.), *Growing points in ethology* (pp. 303-317). Cambridge: Cambridge University Press.

Judge, T. A., Bono, J. E., Ilies, R., and Gerhardt, M. W. (2002). Personality and leadership: A qualitative and quantitative review. *Journal of Applied Psychology, 87,* 765-780.

Kagel, J. H., and Roth, A. E. (Eds.). (1995). *The handbook of experimental economics.* Princeton, NJ: Princeton University Press.

Kroeber, A. L. (1944). *Configurations of culture growth.* Berkeley and Los Angeles: University of California Press.

Lee, C. (1993). Followership: The essence of leadership. In W. E. Rosenbach and R. L. Taylor (Eds.), *Contemporary issues in leadership research* (pp. 113-121). Oxford: Westview Press.

Lhermitte, F. (1986). Human autonomy and the frontal lobes. II. Patient behavior in complex and social situations. The 'environmental dependency syndrome.' *Annals of Neurology, 19,* 335-343.

Lykken, D. T. (1982). Research with twins: The concept of emergenesis.*Psychophysiology, 19,* 361-373.

Maynard-Smith, J. (1982). *Evolution and the theory of games.* Cambridge: Cambridge University Press.

Maynard-Smith, J., and Price, G. (1973). The logic of animal conflict. *Nature, 246,* 15-18.

Mazur, A. (1973). A cross-species comparison of status in small established groups. *American Sociological Review, 38,* 513-530.

Meltzoff, A., and Gopnik, A. (1993). The role of imitation in understanding persons anddeveloping a theory of mind. In S. Baron-Cohen, H. Tager-Flusberg, and D. J. Cohen (Eds.), *Understanding other minds: Perspectives from autism* (pp. 335-366). Oxford: Oxford University Press.

Miller, N. E., and Dollard, J. (1941). *Social learning and imitation.* New Haven: Yale University Press.

Monaghan and Glickman. (1992). Hormones and aggressive behavior. In J. Becker, S. Breedlove, and D. Crews (Eds.), *Behavioral endocrinology* (pp. 261-285). Cambridge MA: MIT Press.

Mumford, L. (1966).The Myth of the Machine. NY: Harcourt, Brace and World.

Mumford, M. D., Zacarro, S. J., Harding F. D., Jacobs, T. O., and Fleishman, E. A. (2000).Leadership skills for a changing world: Solving complex social problems. *Leadership Quarterly, 11,* 11-35.

Murdock, G. P. (1967). *Ethnographic atlas.* Pittsburgh: University of Pittsburgh Press.

Murray, C. (2003). *Human accomplishment: The pursuit of excellence in the arts and* sciences, 800BC to 1950. New York: Harper Collins.

Parker, S. T., and Gibson, K. R. (1991). *"Language" and intelligence in monkeys and apes.* Cambridge: Cambridge University Press.

Pfeiffer, J. (1982). *The creative explosion: An inquiry into the origins of art and religion.* New York: Harper and Row.

Piaget, J. (1945/1962). *Play, dreams, and imitation in childhood.* New York: Norton. (Original work published 1945)

Plutarch. (2001). *Plutarch's lives* (Vols. 1 and 2; paperback ed.). A. Hugh Clough (ED) New York: Modern Library.

Premack, D., and Premack, A. (1995). Origins of social competence. In M. Gazzaniga (Ed.), *The cognitive neurosciences* (pp. 205-218). Cambridge, MA: MIT Press.

Rappaport, R. (1999). *Ritual and religion in the making of humanity.* Cambridge: Cambridge University Press.

Rizzolatti, G., Fogassi, L., and Gallese, V. (2001). Neurophysiological mechanisms underlying the understanding and imitation of action. *Nature Reviews Neuroscience, 2*(9), 661-670.

Ross, E. D., Homan, R. W., and Buck, R. (1994). Differential hemispheric lateralization of primary and social emotions. *Neuropsychiatry, Neuropsychology, and Behavioral Neurology, 7,* 1-19.

Ruby, P., and Decety, J. (2001). Effect of subjective perspective taking during simulation of action: A PET investigation of agency. *Nature Neuroscience, 4*(5), 546-550.

Russon, A. E. (1997). Exploiting the expertise of others. In A. Whiten and R. W. Byrne (Eds.), *Machiavellian intelligence II: Extensions and evaluations* (pp. 174-206). Cambridge: Cambridge University Press.

Searle, J. R. (1969). *Speech acts.* Cambridge: Cambridge University Press.

Searle, J. R., and Vanderveken, D. (1985). *Foundations of illocutionary logic.* Cambridge: Cambridge University Press.

Simonton, D. K. (1994). *Greatness: Who makes history and why.* New York: Guilford Press.

Simonton,D. K.(1995).Personality and intellectual predictors of leadership.In D. H. Saklofske and M. Zeidner (Eds.), *International handbook of personality and intelligence* (pp. 739-757). New York: Plenum.

Simonton,D. K.(1999).*Origins of genius: Darwinian perspectives on creativity.* New York: Oxford University Press.

Smith, S., Arnett, P., and Newman, J. (1992). Neuropsychological differentiation of psychopathic and nonpsychopathic criminal offenders. *Personality and Individual Differences, 13,* 1233-1243.

Sperber, D., and Wilson, D. (1995). *Relevance: Communication and cognition* (2nd ed.). Oxford: Basil Blackwell.

Sperber, D., and Wilson, D. (2002). Pragmatics, modularity and mind-reading. *Mind and Language, 17,* 3-23.

Strawson, P. (1964). Identifying reference and truth-value. *Theoria, 30,* 96-118. (Reprinted from *Logico-linguistic papers*, pp. 75-95, by P. Strawson, 1971, London: Methuen)

Svare, B. (Ed.). (1983). *Hormones and aggressive behavior.* New York: Plenum Press.

Tomasello, M., Kruger, A. C., and Ratner, H. H. (1993). Cultural learning. *Behavioral and Brain Sciences, 16,* 495-552.

Tooby, J., and Cosmides, L. (1988). Evolutionary psychology and the generation of culture. Part I. Theoretical considerations. *Ethology and Sociobiology, 10,* 29-49.

Townsend, J. (1993). Gender differences in mate preferences among law students. *Journal of Psychology, 127,* 507-528.

Trivers, R. L. (1971). The evolution of reciprocal altruism. *The Quarterly Review of Biology, 46,* 35-57.

Vrij, A. (2000). *Detecting lies and deceit: The psychology of lying and the implications for professional practice.* West Sussex, England: John Wiley and Sons Ltd.

Weber, M. (1946). *For Max Weber: Essays in sociology.* New York, NY: Oxford University Press.

Whiten, A., and Byrne, R.W. (1997). *Machiavellian intelligence II: Extensions and evaluations.* Cambridge: Cambridge University Press.

Zacarro, SJ, Kemp, C. and Bader, P. (2004). Leader traits and attributes. In: The Nature of Leadership. (J Antonikas, AT Cianciolo and RJ Sternberg. Eds.), Sage Publications: Thousand Oaks, CA, Pps. 101-124.

Zentall, T. R., and Galef, B. G., Jr. (1988). *Social learning: Psychological and biological perspectives.* Hillsdale NJ: Lawrence Erlbaum Associates.

INDEX

E

F

J

K

L

M

T

U

V

W

Y